CAMBRIDGE LIBRARY COLLECTION

Books of enduring scholarly value

British and Irish History, General

The books in this series are key examples of eighteenth- and nineteenth-century historiography which show how centuries of political, social and economic change were interpreted during the height of Britain's power. They shed light on the understanding of dynasty, religion and culture that shaped the domestic, foreign and colonial policy of the British empire.

Anecdotes and Traditions, Illustrative of Early English History and Literature, Derived from Ms. Sources

A Fellow of the Society of Antiquaries, William John Thoms (1803–85) pursued literary and bibliographical interests and conversed with the likes of Thomas Macaulay and Charles Dickens. Most notably, he coined the term 'folklore' in 1846 and founded the scholarly periodical Notes and Queries in 1849. This work, containing a selection from the 'Merry Passages and Jests', collected by a Norfolk gentleman, Sir Nicholas L'Estrange (1604–55), with shorter extracts from the anecdotes of John Aubrey, and a manuscript by one John Collet, was prepared by Thoms for the Camden Society in 1839. Thoms had compiled over 600 stories recorded by L'Estrange, but only 141 were though suitable for printing, the others being 'unfit for publication' because of their coarseness. The collection is preceded by a biographical note on L'Estrange and his family by the publisher John Gough Nichols. Other works by Thoms are also reissued in this series.

T0370589

Cambridge University Press has long been a pioneer in the reissuing of out-of-print titles from its own backlist, producing digital reprints of books that are still sought after by scholars and students but could not be reprinted economically using traditional technology. The Cambridge Library Collection extends this activity to a wider range of books which are still of importance to researchers and professionals, either for the source material they contain, or as landmarks in the history of their academic discipline.

Drawing from the world-renowned collections in the Cambridge University Library and other partner libraries, and guided by the advice of experts in each subject area, Cambridge University Press is using state-of-the-art scanning machines in its own Printing House to capture the content of each book selected for inclusion. The files are processed to give a consistently clear, crisp image, and the books finished to the high quality standard for which the Press is recognised around the world. The latest print-on-demand technology ensures that the books will remain available indefinitely, and that orders for single or multiple copies can quickly be supplied.

The Cambridge Library Collection brings back to life books of enduring scholarly value (including out-of-copyright works originally issued by other publishers) across a wide range of disciplines in the humanities and social sciences and in science and technology.

Anecdotes and Traditions, Illustrative of Early English History and Literature, Derived from Ms. Sources

EDITED BY WILLIAM J. THOMS

CAMBRIDGE
UNIVERSITY PRESS

University Printing House, Cambridge, CB2 8BS, United Kingdom

Cambridge University Press is part of the University of Cambridge.
It furthers the University's mission by disseminating knowledge in the pursuit of
education, learning and research at the highest international levels of excellence.

www.cambridge.org
Information on this title: www.cambridge.org/9781108078030

© in this compilation Cambridge University Press 2017

This edition first published 1839
This digitally printed version 2017

ISBN 978-1-108-07803-0 Paperback

ANECDOTES AND TRADITIONS,

ILLUSTRATIVE OF

EARLY ENGLISH HISTORY AND LITERATURE,

DERIVED FROM MS. SOURCES.

EDITED BY WILLIAM J. THOMS, Esq. F.S.A.

" They are *Mucrones Verborum*, pointed speeches.   Cicero prettily calls them *Salinas*, salt pits, that you may extract salt out of and sprinkle it where you will.   They serve to be interlaced in continued speech : they serve to be recited, upon occasion, of themselves : they serve, if you take out the kernel of them, and make them your own."—LORD BACON.

LONDON:

PRINTED FOR THE CAMDEN SOCIETY,

BY JOHN BOWYER NICHOLS AND SON, PARLIAMENT STREET.

M.DCCC.XXXIX.

COUNCIL

OF

THE CAMDEN SOCIETY,

FOR THE YEAR ENDING MAY 1st, 1839.

President,
THE RIGHT HON. LORD FRANCIS EGERTON, M.P.

THOMAS AMYOT, ESQ. F.R.S. Treas. S.A.

JOHN BRUCE, ESQ. F.S.A. *Treasurer.*

JOHN PAYNE COLLIER, ESQ. F.S.A.

CHARLES PURTON COOPER, ESQ. Q.C., D.C.L., F.R.S., F.S.A.

T. CROFTON CROKER, ESQ. F.S.A., M.R.I.A.

THE REV. JOSEPH HUNTER, F.S.A.

SIR FREDERICK MADDEN, K.H., F.R.S., F.S.A.

SIR THOMAS PHILLIPPS, BART., F.R.S., F.S.A.

THOMAS STAPLETON, ESQ. F.S.A.

EDGAR TAYLOR, ESQ. F.S.A.

WILLIAM J. THOMS, ESQ. F.SA. *Secretary.*

THOMAS WRIGHT, ESQ. M.A. F.S.A.

PREFACE.

In submitting to the Members of the Camden Society the following Anecdotes and Traditions, the Editor feels called upon, before proceeding to describe the sources from which they are derived, to explain the motives which induced him to suggest to the Council the propriety of the present publication ; a suggestion acceded to with a kindness which calls forth his best thanks.

In the first place, then, it appeared to the Editor very desirable that the Society should follow the example set them by Chaucer, whose intermixture of lighter matters, amidst the graver portions of his " Canterbury Tales," has been the subject of frequent and well deserved encomium ; so that those Members of the Society who think Minerva looks most bewitching when her face is dimpled with a smile, may be allowed an occasional glimpse of their divinity in that mood which they deem her happiest.

In the next place, the delight with which the few works of a similar character, existing in English Literature, such

as Selden's Table Talk, Bacon's Apophthegms, Spence's Anecdotes, and though last not least in our dear love, Camden's
Remains, have been perused by innumerable readers, convinced
him that a volume of " *Camdeniana*," even though it should
be of far inferior merit to its admirable prototypes, would not
be without its admirers.   He was of course aware that the
scattered anecdotes to be found in its pages, would by many
be looked upon as trifling contributions to our stores of knowledge, scarcely as bricks from which great buildings might be
made, scarcely perhaps as the straws necessary to make the
bricks.   Yet on the other hand he felt persuaded, that these
materials, trifling as they seemed, were worthy of preservation,
and capable of being turned to good account.   Had he had
any scruples upon this point, they must have been removed by
the following passage from the pen of Dr. Southey, which he
begs to quote as a justification for the appearance of the present work, to those who may consider such justification called
for.   Dr. Southey having had occasion to speak of an anecdote of Cromwell's having in his youth quarrelled with Prince
Charles, then Duke of York, beaten him and made his nose
bleed, which is related by Mr. Noble as one of the Traditions
of Hinchinbrook, proceeds, in his usual sound common-sense
manner, to observe :

" Such anecdotes, relating to such a man, even though
they may be of doubtful authenticity, are not unworthy of
preservation.   The fabulous history of every country is part
of its history, and ought not to be omitted by later and more

enlightened historians; because it has been believed at one time, and while it was believed it influenced the imagination, and thereby, in some degree, the opinions and character of the people. *Biographical Fables*, on the other hand, are worthy of notice, because they show in what manner the celebrity of the personage, in whose honour or dishonour they have been invented, has acted upon his countrymen."

The Editor is content to rest his defence of the biographical portion of the following volume upon this passage. With regard to that remaining part of it which is devoted to the superstitions of the country, he feels that no apology is necessary. Of what importance an apparently trifling fact may become—in illustration of the source of National Mythology—in confirmation or disproval of the speculations of the learned upon that point,—or by comparison with cognate Traditions—all who have studied such subjects will readily admit. And, when he adds that he has been assured by very competent authority that two or three of the facts contained in the second part of this work will, in all probability, be regarded by that profound scholar Dr. Jacob Grimm, the learned author of the " Deutsche Mythologie," as of the first importance in deciding a point very essential to a right knowledge of that subject, he thinks he shall have satisfied his readers that he has not misused the confidence reposed in him by the Council, when they entrusted him with the compilation of this volume.

The first part of the following collection is entirely derived from the Harleian MS. No. 6395, entitled " Merry Passages

and Jests," compiled by Sir Nicholas Lestrange, of Hunstanton, from the communications of his friends, and containing
upwards of six hundred articles, of which the greater portion
are unfit for publication. Of this manuscript further particulars are here rendered unnecessary by the kindness of John
Gough Nichols, Esq. F.S.A. who has obligingly presented the
Editor with the very elaborate and interesting account of its
author, his relations and associates, which will be found immediately following this Preface, and for which and many
other friendly offices performed during the progress of the
present volume, he begs to offer his warmest acknowledgments.

The Second Part is derived from the Lansdowne MS. No.
231, written by the well-known John Aubrey, and containing
his materials (with some subsequent additions by Dr. White
Kennett, Bishop of Peterborough,) for a work, the publication
of which he had contemplated under the title of "*Remains of
Gentilism and Judaism,*" and in which, it appears, he had proposed to draw a parallel between the Superstitions of Greece
and Rome, and those of his own country, finding the records,
or rather traces, of the former in the works of their Poets,
and collecting his English stores from the communications of
his friends. Many interesting passages of this manuscript
have been already transferred by Sir Henry Ellis to his edition
of Brand's Popular Antiquities ; these, with one exception,
that of the Funeral Dirge, have been omitted in the present
work, but, combined with those here printed, may be said to
comprise everything deserving of publication, contained in the
volume.

The Third and certainly least important part of the present Collection, has been derived from No. 3890 of the Additional MSS. in the British Museum, the commonplace-book of a Mr. John Collet, as we learn from the following inscription, which is most beautifully written on its first page:

JOHANNES COLLET,

FILIUS

THOMÆ COLLET,

PATER

THOMÆ, GULIELMI ET JOHANNIS

OMNIUM SUPERSTES,

NATUS

QUARTO JUNII 1633,

DENASCITURUS

QUANDO DEO VISUM FUERIT,

INTERIM HUJUS PROPRIETARIUS.

Of Mr. John Collet no further particulars than those he has himself furnished have been obtained. But it is probable he was related to " Old Mr. Collet," of the Record Office in the Tower, who is spoken of by Anthony Wood, in his memoir of Sir William Dugdale.

In submitting the selection which he has made, the Editor has endeavoured to turn the several articles of which it consists to as good an account as his abilities would admit, by identifying the parties, illustrating the customs, and showing, as far as possible, the existence of parallel superstitions. He may, perhaps, in some instances, be considered as having given " an intolerable deal of sack " to the " one half-penny-worth of bread ; " but it will, he believes, in most cases, be found upon examination that he had a purpose in doing so, a method, as it were, in his madness, and that it was not done to make a parade of his very limited reading, but rather, and that more especially in his notes to the Second Part, to call the attention of inquirers to sources of information, which are as yet too little known to the antiquarian students of this country.

It now only remains for the Editor to acknowledge his debt of gratitude to his esteemed friend John Bruce, Esq. F.S.A. for his prompt and valuable assistance upon this as upon many other occasions. He knows that, had he consulted the inclination of that gentleman, these acts of kindness must have been passed over in silence ; but he really cannot consent to do so much violence to his own feelings.

WILLIAM J. THOMS.

NOTICES

OF

SIR NICHOLAS LESTRANGE, BART.

AND HIS FAMILY CONNEXIONS.

COMMUNICATED BY J. G. NICHOLS, ESQ. F. S A.

THE person who now makes his first appearance as a posthumous author, after a lapse of nearly two centuries from the days in which he lived, is one for whose biography the apparent materials are exceedingly scanty, and whose mere existence as a country gentleman of Norfolk is almost all that is recorded. It requires, indeed, a little research before the reader of the "Merry Passages and Jests," now the MS. Harl. 6395, can satisfy himself of the identity of their collector; for the book contains no contemporary statement that directly specifies his name. But in the course of the volume, and particularly in the catalogue at the end, which gives the authorities from whom the anecdotes were derived, he mentions so many of his relatives, that at length it is fully ascertained that the writer was no other than Sir Nicholas Lestrange, the first Baronet of Hunstanton; the elder brother of a person of considerable reputation at the latter part of the 17th century, in what is now called periodical literature,—that voluminous essayist and political pamphleteer, Sir Roger Lestrange.

Having arrived at this conclusion, we find that several of the anecdotes which are given on the writer's own knowledge, are marked S. N. L.—the first letter being the initial of his title of knighthood, a practice which was usual until the frequent occurrence of more than one baptismal name rendered it ambiguous and uncertain.

Sir Nicholas Lestrange was the representative of a junior branch of the Barons le Strange of Knockyn in Shropshire, which, seated on the manor of Hunstanton in Norfolk, had for many generations occupied a prominent station among the knightly houses of that county. But it is not necessary to enter here into the early history of the family. It will be found detailed at length in the History of Norfolk, and in the Baronetage by Wotton, published in 1741; and its most important points have more recently formed the subject of a memoir by Daniel Gurney, esq. F.S.A. in the XXVth volume of the Archæologia, where a long series of domestic accounts of the household at Hunstanton, during a large portion of the 16th century, have been presented to the world. The present notices will be almost entirely confined to the parties mentioned in the MS. volume which has given rise to these remarks.

Sir Nicholas was born in the year 1603; and during the whole of his life, with the exception of fourteen months, was only a heir apparent. His father Sir Hamon Lestrange, who was knighted at the Tower of London immediately on the arrival of King James the First in the metropolis of his new kingdom, on the 13th March 1603-4; and who was afterwards Sheriff of Norfolk in 1609, and M.P. for that county in 1620; was living until the 31st of May 1654, when he died at the age of seventy-one, and was buried at Hunstanton. His epitaph is characteristic not only of the age in which such quibbling epitaphs were common, but also of the Anecdotist his son, by whom or with whose concurrence we may presume it was inscribed:

" HAMO EXTRANEUS *miles ob.* 31 *Maij* 1654, *ætat. suæ* 71.

In terris Peregrinus eram, nunc Incola cœli.

In heaven at Home, o blessed change !

Who while I was on earth was Strange."

More than thirty of Sir Nicholas's anecdotes are given on the authority of " My Father," or " Mon Pere ; " and a still larger number on that of " My Mother," or " Ma Mere." The latter was Alice, the younger daughter and coheiress of Richard Stubbe, of Sedgford in Norfolk, esq by Anne [a], daughter and heiress of Richard Goding, of Boston, co. Lincoln, esq. which Anne had been previously the wife of John Lestrange, esq. of Sedgford, a younger brother of Hamon Lestrange, esq. of Hunstanton, the grandfather of Sir Hamon. Alice (Sir Nicholas's mother) was baptized at Sedgford, March 6, 1595 [b]; and died on the 26th Nov. 1656.

Besides his father and mother, Sir Nicholas quotes the authority of

D[cr] Stubbe, Nos. 67, 68, 90, 108.
My bro. Ham. Nos. 180, 423.
Broth. Ham. S. No. 277.
My Sist. Ham. No. 353.
My bro. Roger, Nos. 179, 236, 242, 243, 564, 565, 566.
My sister Eliz. No. 262.

Mr. Spring, No. 195, and many between Nos. 201 and 276.
Sir W. Spring, many between No. 202 and the end.
Bro. Spring, many from No. 245 to the end.
The La. Spr. No. 431.

The preferments of Dr. Stubbe might perhaps be found by turning over the pages of the History of Norfolk, but there is no index to the incumbents. He was probably, however, the same with Edmund Stubbe, S.T.P. whose son John died in 1662, aged 60 ; and was buried at Thurton, in that county, the arms on whose tomb agree with those of Stubbe of Sedgford.

The greater part of the very numerous anecdotes furnished by the name of Spring were probably derived from one person, Sir William Spring, Bart. of Pakenham, in Suffolk, who married our author's sister Elizabeth. He is first called " Mr. Spring " before his creation to a

[a] " A wench came to my Grandmother Stubbe to seeke a service," &c No. 358.
[b] Pedigree by Le Neve in the College of Arms : but perhaps we should read 1585. Her epitaph at Hunstanton (in the History of Norfolk, 1809, vol. x. p. 326,) states her age at her death to have been 71 ; in which case she was two years older than her husband, which is not improbable, as she was the daughter of his *great*-aunt.

Baronetcy in 1641, and before his marriage; and probably the earlier anecdotes assigned to " Sir W. Spring " came from his father of the same name, who was knighted in 1610,.and was Sheriff of Suffolk in 1621. Afterwards the son might be called indifferently " Sir W. Spring " or " Brother Spring." The Lady Spring, as she occurs late in the book, is probably the writer's sister; or if she was the *old* Lady Spring, she was Elizabeth, daughter of Sir William Smith, of Theydon Mount in Essex, Knt.

Sir Nicholas's brother, Hamon Lestrange, was baptized at Sedgford on the 29th Aug. 1605. He married Dorothy, daughter of Edmund La-varich, of Upwell in Norfolk, by whom he had Hamon Lestrange, esq. his son and heir, who was living at Pakenham at the period of Sir Edward Bysshe's Visitation of Suffolk in 1664. This brother Hamon was the author of " The Reign of King Charles, an History faithfully and impartially delivered and disposed into Annals," published anonymously, in folio, 1655. He also wrote " An Answer to the Certamen Religiosum, or the Conference between Charles I. and the Marq. of Worcester," 8vo. 1651, which created a controversy with the celebrated Dr. Peter Heylin; [c] and two theological essays, one on the Sabbath, published in 1641; another on the Liturgy, entitled " The Alliances of Divine Offices," fol. 1659; and also a third essay, written to prove " The Americans no Jews," 4to. 1652.

Of Sir Roger Lestrange it will not be necessary to say many words, as there is a long memoir of him in the Biographia Britannica, which has of course been transferred, in part, to other works of a similar nature.[d] It may be remarked, however, in illustration of the anecdote of the " very choice Rose Viole," told on his authority (No. xli.), that his performance on the same instrument, at a private concert held at the house of Mr. Hinckson in St. James's Park, during the course of

[c] See Wood's Athenæ Oxon. by Bliss, ii. 527; iii. 201, 563.

[d] An original portrait of Sir Roger, by Kneller, which it is believed has never been engraved, is in the possession of Richard Frankum, Esq. a member of the Camden Society.

which the Protector Cromwell unexpectedly came in, " and found them playing " (for such was Sir Roger's explanation of the affair), afterwards gained him from his political antagonists the nickname of " Oliver's Fidler." [e] Sir Roger was thirteen years younger than his eldest brother, having been born at Hunstanton Dec. 17, 1616: after incurring various hazards from his political zeal, he lived to the advanced age of eighty-eight, and, dying in 1704, was buried in the church of St. Giles's in the Fields.

According to the usual practice of former times, Sir Nicholas speaks of his wife's relations as his own.   Of these we find

My Wife, Nos. 123, 173, 175, 365, 369, 402, 408.
Lad. Lewkner, No. 294.
Ned Lewkener, Nos. 64, 77, 78, 86, 89.
My Sist. Ka. Lewknor, No. 370.
My Bro. Russell, Nos. 323, 331.
Mr. Russell, Nos. 163, 164.
Ed. Gurney, Nos. 30, 451.
N. Gurney, No. 103.
Ned Gurney, No. 135, 363.
Fra. Gurney, No. 120.
Tho. Gurney, Nos. 99, 271, 273.

My couz. Dol. Gurny, No. 169.
Couz. Dor. Gourny, Nos. 234, 343, 354, 359, 364.
My aunt Nevill, No. 31.
Mr. Wil. Nevill, Nos. 69 to 74.
Mr. H. Nevill, jun. No. 61.
Mr. Catline, No. 28.
My unck. Catline, Nos. 48, 51, 52.
My unck. T. Catline, Nos. 60, 76, 94, 100, 109, 115, 330, 355.
Unck. Rich. Catline, Nos. 79, 159, 447.
My A: Ca: Nos. 114, 118.

Sir Nicholas's wife was Anne, daughter of Sir Edward Lewkenor, of Denham in Suffolk, Knt. an alliance which is peculiarly memorable in the history of the family of Lestrange, as through it their present representative is one of the coheirs of the ancient Barony of Camoys [f]. She was born in the year 1612, and was consequently about

* There is a pamphlet in the British Museum, printed in 1683, attacking him under the title of " The Loyal Observator ; or, Historical Memoirs of the Life and Actions of Roger the Fidler ; alias, The Observator."

f See the case of " Henry Le Strange Styleman, of Hunstanton, in the county of Norfolk, Esq. on his claim to the title and dignity of Baron Camoys," in the House of Lords, Session 1838 ; also the " Minutes of Evidence given before the Committee of Privileges, to whom the Petition of Thomas Stonor, of Stonor, Esq. claiming to be the senior co-heir of the Barony Camoys, was referred." Printed by order of the House of Lords, 1838.

nine years younger than her husband. They were married [g] in the year 1630; and she survived him about eight years, dying on the 15th July 1663, aged 51; having given birth to a very numerous family of sons. Her mother, " Lady Lewkner," was Mary daughter of Sir Henry Neville, of Billingbere in Berkshire. She had been a widow for some years before her daughter's marriage, Sir Edward having died on the 1st May 1618, at the early age of thirty-one. He consequently is not mentioned by Sir Nicholas Lestrange. By her will [h] made in 1642, Lady Lewkenor left " to my eldest daughter the lady Ann le Strange, my coach and fower coachorses, with all to them belonging. All my other goods, plate, jewells, household stuffe, &c. to my three daughters, to be equally devided, viz. the lady Ann le Strange, wife unto Sir Nicholas le Strange, of Hunstanton, barronett; Catherine Calthorpe, wife unto James Calthorpe of East Basham, esq. and Mary Lewknor, my youngest daughter." The lady last-mentioned died an aged spinster in 1678 [i].

" Ned Lewkenor " was this lady's only son, and consequently brother-in-law to our Anecdotist, viz. Edward Lewkenor, of Denham, Esq. who died in 1634, aged twenty-one, leaving by his wife Elizabeth, daughter of Sir William Russell, of Chippenham in Cambridgeshire, Bart. (who had for her second husband Dr. John Gauden, Bishop

---

[g] Their marriage settlement was made by an indenture quadripartite, dated the 25th Aug. 1630, between Sir Hamon Le Strange, of Hunstanton, Knight, and Dame Alice his wife, of the first part; Sir Nicholas Le Strange, Baronet, son and heir apparent of the said Sir Hamon and Alice, of the second part; Dame Mary Lewkenor, the relict of Sir Edward Lewkenor, late of Denham in Suffolk, deceased, Richard Catline, of Lakenham, in the county of the city of Norwich, Esq. and Thomas Catline, of Norwich, gentleman, of the third part; and John Spelman, Esq. son and heir-apparent of Sir Henry Spelman, of Congham, in Norfolk, Knt. and Sir Robert Walpole, of Houghton, co. Norfolk, of the fourth part. This document is printed at length in the Minutes of Evidence mentioned in the last note, pp. 378-391. Among the witnesses to its execution were Fra. Bacon, Valentine Pell, Edward Gourney. The two latter persons will be noticed hereafter ; and Fra. Bacon was, perhaps, " Mr. Bacon the lawyer " mentioned in p. 9 of the present volume, as the Chancellor is duly called " the Lord Verulam " two pages after.

[h] Printed in the Minutes of Evidence (as above), p. 170.

[i] See her will, made in the previous year, ibid. p. 208.

of Worcester), an only child Mary, afterwards married to Horatio first Viscount Townshend.

Whether " My Bro. Russell" was one of this family (in which case the title " brother " must have been quite one of courtesy,) there are not sufficient grounds to form a conclusion : but this mention of the name affords an opportunity of correcting a note in p. 78 of the present volume, in which it is conjectured that the " Francke Russell" of the anecdote No. cxxxix was a son of the Earl of Bedford. He was, in fact, a much more prominent character of the busy times in which he lived. He was the eldest son of Sir William Russell, of Chippenham, and a zealous Parliamentarian, though his next brother Sir William Russell, j who was joint Treasurer of the Navy with Sir Henry Vane, was always steadfast in his loyalty, and suffered imprisonment on that account. " Francke " was returned to the Long Parliament for the county of Cambridge ; k had a Colonel's commission from the Parliament at the breaking out of the war; was made Governor of the Isle of Ely, afterwards of Lichfield, and then of Guernsey and Jersey; and at length, in 1657, was selected by Oliver Cromwell[1] to be a member of his House of Lords. He had succeeded to the title of Baronet on his father's death in 1653-4. Sir Francis Russell survived the Restoration, and died in 1664.

To return from this digression to the other relations of Lady Lestrange :—

j Sir William Russell (the father) was himself Treasurer of the Navy ; and held that office in 1633, at the period of the settlement on the marriage of his daughter with " Ned Lewkenor," which will be found in the Minutes of Evidence on the Camoys Peerage, 1838, p. 371.

k Sir John Potts, mentioned in the same anecdote (see p. 79,) was one of the Members for the county of Norfolk, and took the Solemn League and Covenant.

[1] Three alliances took place between the family of Sir Francis Russell and that of the Protector. His son and heir Sir John married Frances, the Protector's youngest daughter, widow of the Hon. Robert Rich (who died in 1657-8) ; his daughter, Elizabeth Russell, was married (about 1655), to Oliver's younger son Henry, the Lord Lieutenant of Ireland ; and, thirdly, Elizabeth Cromwell, one of the offspring of the last-named couple, was married to William Russell, of Fordham, co. Camb. esq. nephew to Sir Francis.

"My sister Ka. Lewknor" was afterwards the wife of James Calthorpe, Esq. of East Barsham, Norfolk, who was Sheriff of Norfolk in
1643, and whose portrait in military costume (painted in 1640,) is
engraved in the History of Norfolk. He died on the 19th April, 1652,
aged 48; and his widow Katharine, having survived him twenty-five
years, on the 17th Nov. 1677, aged 61.[m] Their son, Sir Christopher
Calthorpe, of East Barsham, K.B., married Dorothy, daughter of Sir
William Spring, of Pakenham, Bart. and niece of Sir Nicholas Lestrange ;
and they, among other children, had a daughter Anne, who was married
to her cousin Sir Thomas Lestrange, the fifth Baronet of Hunstanton,
and died in 1742, s. p. By descent from Mrs. Katharine Calthorpe,
Sir Jacob Astley, of Melton Constable, Norfolk, Bart. is now another
of the coheirs of the barony of Camoys.

Philip Calthorpe, the contributor of many stories to Sir Nicholas
Lestrange's collection, is believed to have been an uncle of James, and
a younger son of Sir James Calthorpe of Cockthorp, Norfolk, who died
in 1614. If so, he was brother of Sir Henry Calthorpe, of Ampton in
Suffolk, and Recorder of London, the ancestor of the present Lord Calthorpe. Philip was of Gressenhale, in Norfolk, where the principal
manor belonged to the Lestranges of Hunstanton ; whether his wife
(whose name, from two different authorities, we gather to have been
Elizabeth Wade) was a relation of that family has not been ascertained, but he named his son Lestrange; and Sir Lestrange Calthorpe,
Knt. became a serjeant at law and King's Serjeant to Charles the
Second; and dying April 5, 1678, was buried at West Barsham.[n]

The Gurneys were Lady Lestrange's maternal cousins; and they
were also more distantly related to Sir Nicholas himself. Martha,
daughter of Sir Edward Lewkenor, of Denham,[o] and aunt of Lady

[m] Epitaphs at East Barsham. See her Will in the Evidence on the Camoys Peerage, 1838,
p. 196 ; witnessed by Elizabeth Spring and Mary Lewkenor (her sister).

[n] See the History of Norfolk, vii. p. 46, for his descendants.

[o] This Sir Edward Lewkenor died and was buried at Denham in 1605. See in Evidence

Lestrange, was married to Thomas Gurney, Esq. of West Barsham, Norfolk, who died in 1614; leaving issue Edward Gurney, Esq. of the same place, who is the "Ned Gurney" of our book. He married Frances Hood, and died in 1641.

Thomas Gurney was a younger brother of Edward, and was living after the Restoration.

"My couz. Dol." or Dorothy Gurney, was sister to "Ned," and died single. Her will was proved in 1641.

Sir Nicholas Lestrange was himself related to the Gurneys, through his great-grandmother Elizabeth Gurney, the wife of Richard Stubbe, Esq. (married 25th Sept. 1561), and the aunt of Thomas Gurney, Esq. already mentioned.ᴾ

Francis Gurney (No. 120) was an uncle of Edward, and a merchant in London. In an account-book at Hunstanton, apparently written by Alice Lady Lestrange, is frequent mention of Francis Gurney the merchant.

"Parson Edmund Gurney," whose facetiousness is exhibited in the Anecdotes xi. and cv. (hereafter pp. 6, 59), was brother to Francis. He was presented to the rectory of Edgefield in Norfolk by his uncle (by marriage) Richard Stubbe, Esq. in the year 1614, and held it until 1620; in which year he was preferred to the rectory of Harpley in the same county, on the presentation of Sir William Yelverton; and he seems to have held the latter benefice until 1648.

Francis Quarles, the Poet of the Emblems, of whom Sir Nicholas

on the Camoys Peerage, p. 160, his funeral certificate, signed by "Thomas Gurnay," among others.

ᴾ " Independently of this connexion through the family of Stubbe, the Gurneys were related to the Lestranges through the Calthorpes and Heydons : and an old pedigree at Hunstanton gives a marriage of Lestrange and Gurney, but I have not met with a confirmation of this. The only coat of arms in glass remaining at Hunstanton Hall, previous to the late alterations, was Lestrange impaling Gourney ; but I think this was intended for Heydon, the arms of which family are nearly similar to those of Gurney." Communication of Daniel Gurney, esq. of North Runcton in Norfolk, F.S.A. to whom the writer begs to acknowledge his obligations for various information. J. G. N.

relates an anecdote (hereafter p. 48.) was a family connection parallel with the Gurneys. His brother Sir Robert Quarles married, for his first wife, Hester, daughter of Sir Edward Lewknor, (at whose funeral in 1605 he was present,) and sister to Mrs. Martha Gurney.[p]

The Nevilles and the Catlyns were the uncles and aunts of Lady Lestrange. Sir Henry Neville, of Billingbere in Berkshire, (the direct ancestor of the present Lord Braybrooke,) married Anne daughter of Sir Henry Killigrew, of Cornwall; which " old Lady Nevill " is mentioned in Anecdote 69 of our MS. They had issue Sir Henry Neville, junior (the authority for Anecdote 61), who married Elizabeth, daughter of Sir John Smith, of Ostenhanger in Kent (" my aunt Nevill "[q] of No. 31); and five daughters, of whom Elizabeth was married to Sir Henry Berkeley, of Yartington, co. Somerset, Knt. (the authority for Nos. 63, 65); Katharine to Sir Richard Brooke, of Norton in Cheshire, Knt. (mentioned in No. 31); Mary to Sir Edward Lewkenor, Knt. and was the Lady Lewkenor already noticed, the mother of Lady Lestrange; and Dorothy to Richard Catlyn, Esq. of Kirkby Cane in Norfolk. Dorothy was of course entitled to the appellation of " My aunt Catlyn " from Lady Lestrange; her husband might himself by courtesy be called " uncle Richard; " but how Thomas (who was his brother) could acquire the title of " uncle Tho. Catline " it is difficult to reconcile with our modern acceptation of such terms of relationship. Both had, however, been parties to the marriage settlement of our Baronet.[r] Thomas Catlyn was then of the City of Norwich, and afterwards of Blofield in Norfolk, Gent.[s] Richard Catlyn, Esq. was a Member of the Long Parliament for the City of Norwich; and was disabled from his senatorial privileges Jan. 22, 1643, for having deserted the service of the House, and attended the King's Convention at Ox-

[p] Pedigree of Lewkenor, and Morant's Essex, i. 68, where the Poet is erroneously named James.

[q] The story told by " My Aunt Nevill " is a very trifling one of her brother-in-law Sir Richard Brooke when a boy.

[r] See the note in p. xvi, *antea*.   [s] History of Norfolk, viii. 35.

ford.   His son Sir Neville Catlyn, Knt. was of Wingfield castle in
Suffolk in 1664.

From the relations of Sir Nicholas's wife we proceed to those of his
mother, Alice Stubbe before mentioned.

S^r Wi. Yel. jun. No. 25.	My coz. Jo. Spelman, Nos. 55, 125, 143,
Sir H. Yel. Lady, No. 23.	422.
My coz. Tyrrell, No. 17.	Clem. Spelman, No. 506.
Dr. Cademan, No. 529.	

Dame Alice Lestrange was the younger daughter and coheir of
Richard Stubbe, Esq.; and her elder sister Dionysia[t] was married to
Sir William Yelverton, of Rougham in Norfolk, who was created a Baronet in 1620, and was Sheriff of that county in 1621.   They had issue
" Sir William Yelverton, junior," who became the second Baronet,
and died on the 9th July 1648.   His wife was Ursula, eldest daughter
of Sir Thomas Richardson, Chief Justice of the King's Bench.   Against
the Chief Justice, Sir Nicholas Lestrange appears to have always cherished very unkindly feelings.   One story to his disadvantage is printed
hereafter, p. 53; another is as follows:

" When Charles Richardson was dead, (younger son of the Lord
Chief Justice, then living,) some were questioning where the body
should be entered: ' Why,' sayes one, ' where should he be buried,
but where his father *lyes*—at Westminster?'   *No.* 101. *Ham. Bozun.*"

There are, besides, two other stories (Nos. 85 and 93, told on
the authorities of " My Father " and " Ham. Bozune"), both tending
to show the unpopularity of the Chief Justice, as they tell of insults
publicly given him, but they are not worth extracting.

Sir William Yelverton, the second Baronet, was succeeded by his

---

[t] It is to this lady that the trifling story told by Sir Henry Yelverton's lady (No. 23),
relates : " Old Sir Will. Yelverton's lady (my aunt) reading the fourteenth verse of Mathew,
the eighth chapter, where Peter's wives mother lay sicke of a feaver, reade that Peter's wives
mother lay sicke of a feather-bedde."

son, a third Sir William, who did not long survive him, dying on the
15th of Nov. 1649, unmarried [u]. Sir Henry Yelverton, knt. was his
uncle, who married Alice, daughter and coheiress of Dr. William Bar-
low, Bishop of Lincoln. This, no doubt, was the " Sir Harry Yelverton's lady," who gave birth to the bon-mot in p. 5 (hereafter); and not
the wife of Sir Henry Yelverton the Attorney-general.

Margaret Yelverton, sister of Sir William and Sir Henry, was married to Thomas Tyrrell, of Gipping in Suffolk, esq.; wherefore we hear
of " Cousin Tyrrell." Anne, another sister, was the wife of Dr. Cademan: upon whose authority we have the following anecdote, which is,
perhaps, worth extracting as illustrating the character of a distinguished
nobleman:

" The Earl of Bedford [x] was a close and wary man for his estate, and
applyde his abilities much to the knowledge of the law; insomuch as
his sister the Lady Carlisle sayd, by way of scoffe, that she knew little
her brother was good for but to speake bawdy in law termes, for it
seemes he had used some lawe-metaphors to her in his discourses."
No. 529, Dr. Cademan.

" My coz. Jo. Spelman " was a more distant kinsman than the Yel
vertons. His mother was a half-sister of the old Lady Yelverton and
the old Lady Lestrange, being Eleanor, the eldest and eventually the
sole heir of John Lestrange, esq. of Sedgford, before-mentioned, the

[u] A monument was erected to him and his father at Rougham by John Bladwell, esq.; see
the anecdote of " *old* Bladwell " in p. 7.

[x] This is William the fifth Earl, who succeeded his father in that title in 1641, and who, in
his old age, was created a Duke by King William the Third in 1694. His sister Margaret was
the wife of James Hay, second Earl of Carlisle of that family. See in Wiffen's Memorials of
the Russells, vol. ii. p. 129, an elaborate eulogy on the " feminine reserve and delicacy " of
her aspect, a character which the present anecdote by no means tends to support. Nor is
her " reserve " exhibited in another anecdote which has recently appeared: " Some say the
Countess of Carlisle gave secret intelligence to the Five Members and Kimbolton of the King's
design, and so they fled into the Cittie." Diary [or rather Common-place-book] of the Rev.
John Ward, 8vo. 1839, p. 152.

first husband of Anne Goding, afterwards Mrs. Stubbe. She was married to Sir Henry Spelman, of Congham in Norfolk, the great legal antiquary, who died in 1641; and their son, our anecdotist's cousin, was Sir John Spelman, of Heydon in Norfolk, who also published a Saxon Psalter, and wrote the Life of Alfred the Great, which was published by Hearne in 1678. He was knighted in 1641; and died at Oxford in 1643.[y]

Clement Spelman, the younger son of Sir Henry, was a masquer in Davenant's Triumphs of the Prince d'Amour, performed at the Middle Temple in 1635, and became Cursitor Baron of the Exchequer at the Restoration. He died in 1679.

We have now only to notice Sir Nicholas Lestrange's more distant paternal cousins, and first those whose consanguinity was derived from his grandmother, Mary, daughter of Sir Robert Bell, Lord Chief Baron of the Exchequer.

Sir Rob. Bell, Nos. 45, 158, 160, 502, 526.	Mi. Hobart, No. 27.
Clem. Bell, Nos. 41, 42.	Nat. Hobart, Nos. 129, 507.
Sir John Hobart, Nos. 58, 59.	My Cous. T. Hobart, No. 29, 49.
Lady Hobart, Nos. 7, 34.	Capt. Hobart, Nos. 84, 508, 510.

" Sir Robert Bell " was grandson of the Chief Baron, and the nephew of Dame Mary Lestrange; a brief biographical note respecting him is given in p. 12.

Sir John Hobart was the eldest son of Sir Henry Hobart, Chief Justice of the Common Pleas, created a Baronet in 1611, by Dorothy, daughter of the Chief Baron Sir Robert Bell, and sister of Dame Mary Lestrange. Sir John was born in 1593, and succeeded his father as a Baronet in 1626. He became a member of the Long Parliament, on a vacancy for the county of Norfolk, and was a party to the Solemn League and Covenant. He died in 1647, having married two wives,

---

[y] See memoirs of Sir John Spelman in Athenæ Oxon. (edit. Bliss,) iii. 62. He was another of the parties to Sir Nicholas Lestrange's marriage settlement, as mentioned in the note, p. xvi.

both the daughters of Earls, Lady Philippe Sydney and Lady Frances Egerton.

Sir Miles Hobart, the second son of the Chief Justice, was of Intwood in Norfolk; he was born in 1595; knighted Aug. 8, 1623; made K. B. at the Coronation of Charles I. As a member of Parliament, he sided with the popular party; and was one of those who resisted the dissolution in 1628-9, by locking the door of the House until a protestation had been carried. For this he endured imprisonment until 1631, and afterwards received £5000, in recompense for his sufferings, from the Long Parliament. He died in 1649, having married Susan daughter of Sir John Peyton, of Iselham in Cambridgeshire, Bart., and leaving issue Sir John Hobart, who became the third Baronet on his uncle's death, and was the direct ancestor of the present Earl of Buckinghamshire.

Of Nathaniel Hobart, we know only that he was the next son, and married Anne Beke; and, besides the three already mentioned, Chief Justice Hobart had two other sons, James and Thomas. The last, from his " judgment of verses " hereafter, p. 6, we may suppose to have been a scholar and poetical critic. The family pedigree states only, that he died without issue. Which brother was the " Captain" does not appear.

Hamon Bozune, Nos. 93, 101.	Mr. Vall. Pell. No. 403.
Tho. Bozune, Nos. 102, 133, 134, 148.	Mr. Pell, Nos. 3, 301 (in which " Mun.
My cozen Harry Mordant, mentioned in	[Edmund] Gourney " occurs.)
No. 15.	Couz. Jo. Pell, No. 540.

Hamon Bozune was a cousin, and derived his Christian name from the family of Lestrange. Roger Bozune, Esq. of Witheringset, the head of one of the oldest families in Norfolk, married Anne, daughter of Sir Hamon Lestrange, the great-grandfather of our Sir Nicholas. Hamon Bozune, his son and heir, married in 1609 Frances, daughter of Sir Thomas Playters of Sotherley in Suffolk; and had issue Thomas, his son and heir, who sold Witheringset to Katharine, widow of James Calthorpe, esq. (our author's sister-in-law), from whom it descended to the Lestrange family.

" My cozen Harry Mordant," mentioned in the anecdote No. VI (31), was, according to the Baronetage of 1741, the brother, not the nephew (as stated in p. 4) of Sir Robert Mordaunt, Bart. of Great Massingham, Norfolk (who died in 1638, which places the story before that time). Henry was of Congham (the same place as the Spelmans), and he married Barbara, daughter of Sir James Calthorpe, of Cockthorp, Norfolk, aunt, it would seem, to James Calthorpe, Esq. Lady Lestrange's brother-in-law. Mrs. Mordaunt survived to the 27th Dec. 1690.[z] Her son Lestrange Mordaunt, Esq. who died in 1691, aged 63, married Barbara, daughter of Richard Catlyn, Esq.[z] already mentioned as " uncle Rich. Catlyn." The Mordaunts were cousins of the house of Hunstanton, in a remarkable manner, for in fact they represented two distinct junior branches of Lestrange (in what way will be seen by a pedigree in Dugdale's Warwickshire, under Walton d'Eyvill, where the family is still seated), and thence arose their Christian name of Lestrange (first borne by Sir Lestrange Mordaunt, the first Baronet) ; but as Harry Mordaunt, the younger brother, is termed " cousin," whilst Sir Robert is not so, it is possible the former may have been regarded in that light, as much from his alliance with the family of Calthorpe, as from his own descent.

Such a supposition is supported by the circumstance of our finding the connexion of " cousin John Pell " to be apparently derived in the same manner. He was the son of Sir Valentine Pell, of Dersingham (a parish adjoining to Congham), by another Barbara (for she cannot have been the same), daughter of Sir James Calthorpe. " Mr. Valentine Pell" (No. 403), was one of the witnesses to our Baronet's marriage settlement, already frequently referred to ; he received the honour of knighthood July 2, 1641 ; was Sheriff of Norfolk in 1645 ; and died in 1658, having survived his son, John Pell, Esq., who died in 1649.[a]

We have now rehearsed the whole of Sir Nicholas Lestrange's rela-

---

[z] Epitaphs at Congham ; Hist. of Norfolk, 1808, viii. 388.
[a] Epitaphs at Dersingham.

tions mentioned in the MS. with the exception of one other cousin, whose genealogical position has not been traced.

Mr. Pament, No. 37.   My couz. Pament, No. 341.

It would here be desirable to return to the personal history of Sir Nicholas Lestrange, were there any materials for that purpose. But beyond the circumstance of his being created a Baronet (during his father's life-time) by patent dated June 1, 1629, the page of history is silent. On the breaking out of the civil war, his father, Sir Hamon, became the governor of the neighbouring town of Lynn on the King's behalf, and defended it when besieged by the Earl of Manchester. On its capitulation, in Sept. 1643, we find Sir Hamon himself retained as one of the hostages,[b] until the performance of the conditions; whilst among the parties to the treaty on the Parliamentarian side, were Col. Russell,[c] and Mr. Philip Calthorpe.

The name of Sir Nicholas Lestrange does not occur in this affair; but in the course of the following year his brother, afterwards Sir Roger made himself conspicuous in an attempt to surprise the town, for which, being seized, he was tried by a court martial, and narrowly escaped with his life, continuing in prison for about five years after.

Though Sir Nicholas's anecdotes do not abound with historical or political information of much importance, there are several towards the end of his collection containing allusions which shew that they were written in the times of " civil discord." In his No. 407 the year 1640 is mentioned (see p. 56), and in No. 502 occurs the year 1642. The two following are particularly impressed with the characteristics of the times.

---

[b] Another was Capt. Clinch, who was the authority for Nos. 531 to 534, 545, 548, and 550 of Sir Nicholas's Anecdotes.

[c] This was either Colonel Francis Russell, already noticed in p. xvii, or his brother Colonel John Russell, an officer who distinguished himself both in the battle of Marston Moor, and in Oliver's army employed against Spain.

" Tobias Fryar,^q a pretended zelote, but true ringleader and head of all factious and schismaticall spiritts in the country, puft up with the pride and strength of his party, would needs be stand to be K^t (or rather K [nave]) of the shire for Norff. but fell most shamefully short and lost it, with many squibs and disgraces : only, for his comfort, a True Disciple of his sayd, ' However, I am sure Mr. Fryar stood for Christ Jesus, for none but reprobates and prophane wretches went against him.'—*No. 553. Dr. Baron.*"

" A regiment of King Charles's horse, in a summer night, yet very darke, casually fell in upon the enemie. The Colonell bared his upper parts to his shirt, charged, routed, chaced, killed most, tooke the rest. One wondering at the defeat and strange execution in the darke, an officer swore they had light enough, for they fought and could distinguish colours by the moonshine of their Commander's shirt.

" *No. 566. Frat. Rog.*"

Before the close of the Protectorate, Sir Nicholas Lestrange died in his 52d year, on the 24th July 1655, and was buried at Hunstanton. His eldest son, Hamon, became the second Baronet,^r but died unmar-

---

^q The time of this political contest was probably the election of the Long Parliament in 1640. Like other political aspirants, Mr. Frere was not easily discouraged, and we find he was actually elected one of the Members for Norfolk to the Short, or Barebones, Parliament of 1653 ; and again to Cromwell's second Parliament in 1654. He was, by purchase, of Redenhall in Norfolk, in the church of which parish is a Latin epitaph recording his death on the 6th Feb. 1655, in his 66th year (see History of Norfolk, 1806, v. 365), and also on his gravestone the following :

" TOBIAS FRERE, Esq. Febr. 6, 1655,
His Corps lye here : his Soule, like to the dove,
Finding small rest below, now rests above."

^r In all the publications on the Baronetage, including Courthope's " Synopsis of the Extinct Baronetage of England," 1835, and Burke's " Extinct and Dormant Baronetcies of England," 1838, this Sir Hamon has been omitted in the descent of the title. The date of his death, and the circumstance of his dying unmarried, were proved before the House of Lords, by the epitaph and arms still on the graavestone in the chancel at Hunstanton. — Minutes of Evidence on the Camoys Peerage, 1838, p. 392.

ried, only eight months after, on the 25th Feb. 1655-6, aged 24; nor was the second son, Sir Nicholas, much longer lived, dying on the 13th Dec. 1669, aged 37. He had, however, two wives, of whom the first was Mary, daughter of John Coke, esq. of Holkham,—the same "great fellow" of whom and his surname Sir Nicholas[s] tells the anecdote, No. xc. p. 61.

The male line of the family became extinct in 1760, on the death of Sir Henry the sixth Baronet, a grandson of the second Sir Nicholas; and its present representative, Henry Lestrange Styleman, Esq. of Hunstanton, is great-grandson of Sir Henry's sister Armine, the wife of Nicholas Styleman, of Snettisham, esq.

[s] The good things which Sir Nicholas has recorded, on the part of his faithful wife, are generally of the most trifling description, and among them is the following, the only one it is believed in which he mentions any of his children: " Fil. me. Nick. reading the chapter of Salutations, Colos. 4, 9, instead of Onesimus, read the word divided thus, with *One simus*, &c."

No. 556. *" My Wife."*

ANECDOTES AND TRADITIONS.

PART I.

NO. I.—SIR DRUE DRURY'S PENMANSHIP.

SIR DRUE DRURY being an ill scribe, having writt a thing very ill, Sir Robert Bell check't him thus:—" Fie, Drue, pr'y-the write so that a man may be saved by the reading on't however."

L'Estrange, No. 2. My Father.

The allusion here made is to the reading, by which criminals proved themselves entitled to the benefit of clergy. The passage actually read upon those occasions is a subject of some doubt; or perhaps the custom differed in various places. The first verse of the 51st Psalm, " *miserere mei*," &c. was often selected, and from that circumstance acquired the name of the neck verse. See a note by Sir Walter Scott to Canto I. of the " Lay of the Last Minstrel." Barrington, however, in his " Observations on the Statutes," p. 350, states, on the authority of Lord Bacon, that the Bishop was to prepare the book, and the Judge was to turn to what part he should think proper.

At present no one can claim the benefit of clergy ; it is entirely abolished by the Act 7 and 8 Geo. IV. c. 28, and every one guilty of felony, whether peer or commoner, layman or spiritual, learned or unlearned, gentle or simple, is made liable to the same punishment.

NO. II.—LADY HOBART'S GRACE.

The Lady Hobart, every one being sett at the table and no body blessing it, but gazing one upon an other, in expectation who should be Chaplaine—"Well," sayes my Lady, "I thinke I must say as one did in the like case, 'God be thanked, nobody will say grace.'"

L'Estrange, No. 7. Lady Hobart.

We have here an anticipation of Sheridan's well-known speech when unexpectedly called upon to say grace at a public dinner,—"What no clergyman present? Thank God for all things!" So true it is that there is nothing new under the sun, and so justly may all professed sayers of good things exclaim with Donatus, the preceptor of St. Jerome, 'Pereant qui ante nos nostra dixerunt!'" One of the most striking cases is that of Talleyrand's well-known apophthegm,—"Language was given to man to conceal his thoughts!" The wily diplomatist, no doubt, *thought* so, and said so; but so had Goldsmith long before him, who tells us in his fifth essay, "that the true use of speech is not so much to express our wants as to conceal them."

Lady Hobart was probably Dorothy, wife of Chief Justice Sir Henry Hobart, daughter of Sir Robert Bell, Lord Chief Baron (see hereafter, No. 24), and aunt of our author.

NO. III.—SHAKSPEARE'S GIFT TO HIS GOD-CHILD.

Shake-speare was god-father to one of Ben Jonson's children, and after the christ'ning, being in a deepe study, Jonson came to cheere him up, and ask't him why he was so melancholy? "No, faith, Ben, (sayes he) not I, but I have been considering a great while what should be the fittest gift for me to bestow upon my god-child, and I have resolv'd at last." "I pr'y the, what?" sayes he. "I' faith, Ben, I 'le e'en give him a douzen good Lattin Spoones, and thou shalt translate them."   *L'Estrange, No. 11. Mr. Dun.*

The MS. from which we are selecting, is the original authority for this anecdote, which we cannot forbear inserting, although we know it has frequently been printed. To omit it would be to destroy the completeness of our selection; and few persons will object to be reminded of so pleasant an illustration of the friendship betwixt the Bard of Avon and rare old Ben. It gives us, as it were, a taste of the combats between the wits of those days, so charmingly described by Beaumont in his letter to Jonson—

> "What things have we seen
> Done at the Mermaid! heard words that have been
> So nimble and so full of subtle flame,
> As if that every one from whom they came
> Had meant to put his whole wit in a jest!

The practice of giving apostle spoons at christenings has been thus described by Steevens in a note to Henry VIII. Act v. sc. 2. "It was the custom formerly for the sponsors at christenings, to offer gilt spoons as a present to the child. These spoons were called *Apostle spoons*, because the figures of the apostles were carved on the top of the handles. Such as were at once opulent and generous gave the whole twelve ; those who were either more moderately rich or liberal escaped at the expense of the four Evangelists, or even sometimes contented themselves with presenting one spoon only, which exhibited the figure of any saint in honour of whom the child received its name."

Shakspeare following this custom, and willing to show his wit, if not his wealth, gave a dozen spoons, not of silver, but of latten, a name formerly used to signify a mixed metal resembling brass, as being the most appropriate gift to the child of a father so learned.

NO. IV.—A LONG SERMON.

There was one preach't in summer and stood two houres ; and one say'd at dinner that 't was a very good sermon, but halfe on't would have done well cold.   *L'Estrange, No.* 12. *Mr. Dun.*

This sermon must have been preached by the Rector of Bibury, of whom Fosbroke, in his British Monachism, speaking on the subject of hour-glasses as furniture for pulpits, tells us, he used always to preach two hours, regularly turning the glass. After the text, the 'squire of the parish withdrew, smoked his pipe, and returned to the blessing.

NO. V.—A SHREWD LOSS.

Doctor Pearne, preaching a funerall Sermon for a townsman's wife in Cambridge (that had beene a very curst wench), told his auditorie that none could judge of the losse of a wife till they had had one ; but beleeve me, brethren, whosoever looseth such a wife as this was, will find it a shrewd losse, a very shrewd losse.

L'Estrange, No. 13. *My Mother.*

Andrew Perne, D.D. Fellow and Master of Peter House and Dean of Ely, was a divine of considerable celebrity. His conformity and zeal for Romanism during the reign of Mary, rendered him suspected and disliked by the Protestant divines of the succeeding reign ; but he had a powerful and generous friend in Archbishop Whitgift, who protected both his person and his fame. "I know him," said the Archbishop, "to be a wise and learned man ; and howsoever the world judgeth of him, and of me for using his familiarity (being by sundry means bound to him, and knowing him very well), yet the day will come, when both they and we shall be known as we are.'' Wood says, he was reported to be '' a man of a facetious nature, yet a great Mecænas of learning.'' He was a liberal benefactor to his college. In the latter part of his life he was much at Lambeth Palace, and dying there April 26, 1589, was buried in Lambeth Church. (Vide Wood's Fasti Oxon. i. 141, Bliss's edition ; and Bentham's Ely, 228.)

The task imposed upon this facetious divine, who, as Fuller relates in his Worthies, was himself killed by a jest, reminds us of what Granger (iv. 219), tells respecting Mother Creswell, a famous procuress of Charles the Second's time, who left by *will* ten pounds for any clergyman that should preach a funeral sermon, and say nothing but what was *well* of her. A preacher was with some difficulty found, who undertook the task ; and concluded a sermon, on the general subject of morality, with saying, '' By the will of the deceased, it is expected that I should mention her, and say nothing but what was *well* of her ; all that I shall say of her, therefore, is this, she was born *well*, she lived *well*, and she died *well*, for she was born with the name of Creswell, she lived in Clerkenwell, and she died in Bridewell.''

NO. VI.—WITHIN AN ACE ON 'T.

A Falconer of Sir Robert Mordant's, not knowing his dogges names, called one of them Cinque whose name was Sice, and my cozen Harry Mordant telling him his error, '' Faith, Sir,'' sayes he, '' 't was well I came so neare : I am sure I was within an Ace on 't.''

L'Estrange, No. 15. Phil. Calth.

Sir Robert Mordaunt, of Massingham, in the county of Norfolk, received the honour of knighthood during the lifetime of his father Sir L'Estrange Mordaunt, who having signalised himself in the reign of Elizabeth, as a military commander in the wars of the Low Countries, and in Ireland, was among the first raised to a baronetcy, being so created 29 June 1611, soon after the institution of the order. He succeeded his father as second baronet in 1627. '' My cousin Harry Mordaunt'' was no doubt Henry, second son of Henry Mordaunt, the brother of Sir Robert.

NO. VII.—A THOROUGH-BRED FOOL.

Jack Paston began one time to jeast upon Capon (who sat very silent and reply'd nothing), and told him merrily he never met with such a dull clay-pated Foole, that could not answere a word, and bade him remember he out-fool'd him once. '' No, faith,'' sayes Capon, '' I were a very Foole indeede, to deak with you at that weapon : I know the straine of the Pastons too well, and you must needs be right-bredd for't, for I am sure your Race has not beene witho't a good Foole these fifty yeares and upward." *L'Estrange, No.* 19. *Mr. Rob. Wallpoole.*

The bitterness of this jest against the Paston family, some of the earlier members of whom evince, in the well-known Collection of Letters, both talent and a fondness for literature, is to be found in the fact, that at an inquisition taken at Norwich Castle, Sept. 3, in the 9th year of James I. the jurors found that Sir Christopher Paston appeared before them personally, and that he was *Fatuus et Idiota*, and had been so for twenty-four years past, &c. (See Blomefield's Norfolk, iii. 698.)

NO. VIII.—A SON-BURNT WOOER.

Sir Henry Yelverton's lady us'd to say of any one that was a widdower, and had a sonne to inheritt his estate, and desir'd a second wife, that nobody would have him he was so sonne-burnt.

L'Estrange, No. 21. *My Mother.*

If this lady was the wife of the celebrated Sir H. Yelverton, who was, in the reign of James I. Solicitor and Attorney-general, and eventually one of the Justices of the Court of Common Pleas, she was the daughter of Robert Beale, Esq. Clerk of the Council, the bearer of the warrant for the execution of the Queen of Scots to Fotheringay.

NO. IX.—DOD THE DECALOGIST.

One Dod, who was nephew to the minister who wrote upon the Commandments, went up and down Paule's Churchyard amongst the Stationers, enquiring for his unkle upon the Commandements.

L'Estrange, No. 26. *Mr. Donne.*

The uncle of this simple gentleman, who was unquestionably the party recorded in Joe Miller as having inquired at the Post Office for a letter ' from his father in the country,' was the celebrated Hebrew scholar John Dod, of Jesus College, Cambridge. He was an eminent puritan divine; and from his Exposition of the Ten Commandments here alluded to, and which he wrote in conjunction with Robert Cleaver, he was commonly called the Decalogist.

Granger, in his Biographical History (i. 370, ed. 1779), tells us, " His Sayings have been printed in various forms; many of them, on two sheets of paper, are still to be seen pasted on the walls of cottages. An old woman in my neighbourhood told me, ' that she should have gone distracted for the loss of her husband, if she had been without Mr. Dod's Sayings in the house.' "

NO. X.—SOBER CRITICISM.

Tho. Hobart, delivering his judgment of verses that were written in sacke and yet scarce sence, [said] that it was impossible to understand them unlesse a man were first drunke.

L'Estrange, No. 29. My Coz. T. Hobart.

Sack was the Poet's drink; and Hobart's opinion in favour of lines written in Sack was that generally entertained. In a Poem " Upon the Vertue of Sack," written by F. Beaumont, he declares of " sprightly sack," that

——————————— " It can
Create a brain, even in an empty pan."

Jonson, as is well known, considered his Volpone, Alchemist, and Silent Woman his best works, as owing their excellence to the influence of good sack; while the " Devil is an Ass " was written, he says, "when I and my boys drank bad wine at the Devil."

NO. XI.—A MATHEMATICIAN DEFINED.

Edm. Gurney used to say that a mathematitian is like one that goes to markett to buy an axe to breake an egg.

L'Estrange, No. 30.   Ed. Gurney.

The following is Fuller's account of the perpetrator of this satire upon mathematics :

" Edmond Gourney, born in this county [Norfolk], was bred in Queen's and Bene't Colledge in Cambridge, where he commenced Bachelour of Divinity, and afterwards was beneficed in this shire.   An excellent scholar, who could be *humorous*, and would be *serious*, as he was himself disposed; his *humours* were never profane towards *God*, or injurious towards his *neighbours;* which premised none have cause to be *displeased*, if in his fancies he•pleased himself.   Coming to me in Cambridge when I was studying, he demanded of me the subject whereon I studied.   I told him, ' I was collecting the witnesses of the truth of the Protestant religion through all ages, even in the depth of Popery, conceiving it feasible, though difficult, to evidence them.'   ' It is a needless pains,' said he, ' for I know that I am descended from Adam, though I cannot prove my pedigree from him.'   And yet, reader, be pleased to take notice he was born of as good a family as any in Norfolk.   His book against Transubstantion, and another on the Second Commandment, are learnedly and judiciously written.   He died in the beginning of our Civil War."

NO. XII.—THE FOOL NO FOOL.

The Lord North begged old Bladwell for a foole (though he could never prove him so), and having him in his custody as a lunatick, he carried him to a gentleman's house one day that was a neighbour. The Lord North and the gentleman retired a while to private discourse, and left Bladwell in the dining-room, which was hung with a fair hanging. Bladwell walked up and down, and viewing the imagery spied a foole at last in the hanging, and, without delay, draws his knife, flies at the foole, cuts him clean out, and lays him on the floor. My Lord and the gentleman coming in again, and finding the tapestrie thus defaced, he asks Bladwell what he meant by such a rude uncivil act: he answered, "Sir, be content, I have rather done you a courtesy than a wrong, for if ever my Lord North had seen the fool there, he would have begged him, and so you might have lost your whole suit."

L'Estrange, No. 32. My Mother.

" *To beg a man for a fool,*" was to apply to the Crown for the custody of his lands and person, he having been found *purus idiota* by a jury. (*Vide* Blackstone's Comment. book i. ch. viii. ; and Nares's Glossary, *voce* Beg.) The biographer of Lord Keeper Guildford, who was probably a grandson of the Lord North referred to in the anecdote, gives a *bon môt* of Charles II. which proves the commonness of the practice. " It is very strange," said the witty monarch, " that every one of my friends keeps a tame knave." (Lives of the Norths, ii. 247.) William Bladwell, esq. living temp. Jas. I. was possessed of large estates at Grimston and elsewhere in Norfolk (see the History of that county by Blomefield and Parkin) ; and to him or one of his family this anecdote must relate.

NO. XIII.—THE GOLDEN FLEECE.

Old Lambe of Burry us'd to goe very brave in apparell, and King James seeing him one day in the field a-hunting, so glittering and radiant as he eclips't all the Court, the King ask't what he was. One of his followers told him it was one Lambe. " Lambe," sayes the King,

" I knowe not what kind of Lambe he is, but I am sure he hath a good fleece on his backe."   *L'Estrange, No. 33. Mr. Alderedge.*

I have not found any other trace of this " Lambe of Bury." There was a family of that name at Ufford in the same county; and several of them were especial benefactors to the church there. " Their names," remarks Weever, " with the pictures of lambs, are depenciled in many places of the wood-work and ceiling of the church." (Fun. Mon. p. 490.)

NO. XIV.—" AN OLD COURTIER OF THE QUEEN'S."

Mrs. Ratcliffe, an old Courtier in Queen Elizabeth's time, told a Lord, whose conversation and discourse she did not like, that his witte was like a custard, nothing good in it but the soppe, and when that was eaten you might through away the rest.

L'Estrange, No. 34. Lady Hobart.

Mrs. Mary Ratclyffe was one of the Queen's Maydens of Honour as early as New Year's day 1561-2; and she was still living to offer a gift to her Royal Mistress on New Year's day 1599-1600 ; so she is with justice termed, " an old courtier " of the Queen. (See Nichols's Progresses, &c. of Queen Elizabeth; Index to New Year's Gifts.) She was a daughter of Sir Humphrey Ratcliffe of Elstow in Bedfordshire, a younger son of Robert Earl of Sussex. (MS. Harl. 2040, f. 173.)

NO. XV.—RECONCILING THE FATHERS.

The Deane of Gloucester, having some merry divines at dinner with him one day, and amongst other discourses, they talking of reconciling the Fathers in some points, he told them he could show them the best way in the world to reconcile them in all points of difference : so after dinner he carryed them into his study and shew them all the Fathers classically ordered, with a quarte of sacke betwixt each of them.

L'Estrange, No. 36. Mr. Garnons.

Could this merry divine, who thus availed himself of the well-known *love-compelling* properties of wine, have been Dr. Richard Field, who is again referred to in No. 25 of this Collection ?

NO. XVI.—SMALL BEER.

One used to say of very small beere, that it was but strong water at the best. *L'Estrange, No.* 39. *N. Kett.*

NO. XVII.—MR. BACON THE LAWYER.

Mr. Bacon the lawyer sayde of Mr. Pooly, a wrangling, dunsicall parson, that his sunne-burnt face shew'd he look't more upon the ayre and a tithe-sheave then on his booke.

L'Estrange, No. 43. *My Father.*

Neither this, nor any other of the sayings of this great man recorded in the MS. from which these anecdotes are derived, appears in the Collection of his Apothegms which I have consulted, namely, that published in 1658, in 12mo.

NO. XVIII.—JUDAS'S PAY.

At the Lecture at St. Gregorie's in Norwich the ministers had 2*s.* 6*d.* a sermon, whereupon Mr. Legate, when he preach't, say'd they gave them Judas his pay, which was 30 pence.

L'Estrange, No. 46. *Mr. Legate.*

The Mr. Legate here alluded to is probably the same with the intruder upon the rectory of Barnham in Suffolk, upon the ejection of William Crofts, D.D. brother to the Lord Crofts, about the year 1644. He is thus noticed in Walker's Sufferings of the Clergy : " His (Crofts') successor at Barnham was one Legate, who had personated Ignoramus in Cambridge, when that play was acted there before his Majesty King James I. and continued ever after a *Perfect Comedian* in the pulpit ; several stories of which kind I could let the reader know, were it worth the while. Though he had never paid Dr. Crofts the Fifths any more than once, yet the Dr. generously proffer'd him £50 a year after he was re-possest of his living in 1660, on condition he would continue there and serve the cure : but, having been instrumental in bringing K. Charles I. to the block, he was forced to fly beyond the seas, and settled in Maryland ; the Governor of which place told Dr. Crofts (who met him one day by chance, and enquired after Mr. Legate) that he had taken him into custody the very morning he came away, for heading a faction ; and, as it seems, endangering a tumult there."—Legate had probably personated Ignoramus, but certainly not when it was acted before the King, on its first production : the character was then sustained by Mr. Thomas Parkinson, of Clare-hall. (Nichols's Progresses, &c. of King James the First, vol. iii. p. 52.)

NO. XIX.—MANNERS MAKE THE MAN.

The Earle of Carlile was commending one of his new acquaintance, and sayde that he did like him as well as any man that ever he convers't with, and thought him every way as absolute; "but," sayes he, "when we went to dinner, and I perceived that he beganne to draw a knife (the cognizance of a clowne) out of his pockett, I beganne at that instant to abhominate and hate him, and could never endure the sight of him after." *L'Estrange, No. 55. My Co. Jo. Spelman.*

The nobleman here referred to was Sir James Hay, who accompanied King James I. from Scotland. Being a younger son of a Scottish family (since Earls of Kinnoul), he received, what was often in those days a younger son's only portion, the advantage of a French education. He always continued one of the King's principal favourites of his own countrymen; and about the period of his first marriage, with the heiress of Lord Denny in 1607, was honoured with the unexampled dignity of a titular Baron, without a seat in Parliament; afterwards, in 1615, he was created a Baron by patent, in 1618 Viscount Doncaster, in 1622 Earl of Carlisle, and in 1625 was made a Knight of the Garter. His second wife was a daughter of the Earl of Northumberland. He was one of the most ostentatious and expensive courtiers of his own or any other age. The pages of Osborne, Wilson, &c. relate several instances of his vain profusion: and in confirmation of the fastidiousness implied in the present anecdote, may be mentioned Osborne's account of his " ante-suppers," which were used only to feast the eye, and then " in a manner thrown away, and fresh set on to the same height, having only this advantage of the other, that it was hot."

NO. XX.—AN AMBASSADOR'S GALLANTRY.

The Earle of Carlile going to a great lady to know her commands, before he went over into France, she told him she had a letter for one of his servants. "Then I beseech you, Madam," sayes he, "let me know which of them it is, that I may have the honour to be his servant." *L'Estrange, No. 485. Mr. Smith.*

The Earl of Carlisle was twice sent Ambassador Extraordinary to France, in 1616 and 1622: and intermediately to the Emperor in 1619. On the first occasion, in particular, his excessive magnificence and expenditure became the theme of universal astonishment. Wilson gives a long account of it, which is confirmed in the contemporary letters of Mr. John Chamberlain (see Nichols's Progresses, &c. of King James I. vol. iii. pp. 177, 183 et seq.)

" The Lady Haddington," writes Chamberlain, " hath bestowed a favour upon him that will not easily fall to the ground ; for she says the flower and beauty of his embassy (1616) consists in three mignards, three dancers, and three fools, or buffoons. The mignards are himself, Sir Harry Rich [afterwards Earl of Holland], and Sir George Goring [afterwards Earl of Norwich] ; the dancers, Sir Gilbert Hoghton, Auchmouty, and Abercromby ; the fools or buffoons are Sir Thomas Jermyn, Sir Ralph Sheldon, and Thomas Badger." (Ibid. 177.)

The Earl of Carlisle died on the 25th of April 1636, and was buried in St. Paul's Cathedral. Clarendon has given a long character of him, in the course of which it is stated, that he wholly ran through £400,000 which he had received from the Crown.

NO. XXI.—LORD BACON.

The Lord Verulam used to say, that he loved to have his throate cut with a razour, and not with a saw ; intimating the smooth and keene oyly knaverie of some, and the ragged, rough, and rude knaverie of others.   *L'Estrange, No. 58. Sir Jo. Hobart.*

NO. XXII.—ONE GOOD TURN DESERVES ANOTHER.

Sir Martin Stuteville's father riding abroade one day, with him attending on him, he rode by the nurse's house that over-laide his eldest sonne, at which time the nurse stoode at the doore : " Looke you there, Martin," sayde his father, " there stands she that made you an elder brother." " Is that she, Sir," sayes he, " marry, God's blessing on her hart for it ! " and presently gallopps up to her and gives her a couple of shillings.   *L'Estrange, No. 60. My Uncle T. Cattline.*

The Stutevilles were a Suffolk family, and long resident at Dalham, in that county ; one of them, probably the father, mentioned in the above anecdote, " continewed and kept hospitalitye," according to an inscription to his memory in Dalham Church, " in the mannor place here forty years together." Sir Henry Ellis has published, in his Collection of Original Letters, many amusing extracts from various news letters addressed to Sir Martin Stuteville by Mr. Joseph Mead, and extant in the Harleian MSS. 389 and 390.

NO. XXIII.—LIKE CAUSES SHOULD PRODUCE LIKE EFFECTS.

Hacklewitt and another drinking hard at the Miter Taverne, and wanting attendance, when the chamberlaine came up, in a madde

humour tooke him up and coyted him downe to the bottome of the
stayres, and almost broke his necke; the fellow complaines, his master
comes and expostulates the cause. " Why," sayes Hacklewitt, " when
we wanted our wine we threw downe a quartt, and presently we had a
pottle came up, and I expected a cast of chamberlaines upon the
throwing downe of this, for none would come with a call, therefore we
thought a knock was the only summons."

L'Estrange, No. 77. Ned Lewkenor.

The only further information which I have to offer, with regard to Hacklewit, is contained
in another anecdote from the same Collection, No. 88, where we are told, on the authority
of Dr. Stubbe, that " Hacklewitt was Doctor Topham's puple, and his tutor was saying to him
one day, (having reproved him for his dissolute courses), ' Well, th' art a very wretch; for I
am sure I am out of £500 for such as thou art, and never drunke for 't.' ' That 's a proper
peece of business indeed,' sayes Hacklewit, ' why I have druncke £500, and never payd
for 't.' "

The Doctor Topham here alluded to, is most probably that Anthony Topham, Dean of
Lincoln, who is mentioned by Anthony Wood, as having " died in the rebellious times."

NO. XXIV.—A CONCENTRATION OF TALENT.

Sir Rob. Bell, being in company with Sir J. Hobart, Sir Cha. Grosse,
&c. in a merry humour would goe make his will, and give every man a
legacie; but when he came to Mr. Paston, sayes he, " I know not
what to bestow on the : my witt I shall not neede for thou must needs
be well stor'd with that, because thou hast the witt of at least three
generations,"—for his great-grandfather, grandfather, and father were
all fooles.   *L'Estrange, No. 79. Unc. Rich. Catline.*

The point of this somewhat unfeeling jest has been already explained in the note to No. vii.
Sir Robert Bell was of Beaupré hall, co. Norfolk, and died in 1639. (See Hist. of
Norfolk, 1807, vii. 460.) He was cousin to the writer of these anecdotes, and to Sir John
Hobart, Knt. and Bart. who was the son and heir of Sir Henry Hobart, Lord Chief Justice,
by Dorothy, daughter of Sir Robert Bell, Lord Chief Baron, before-mentioned under No. II.
Sir Charles Grosse, or Le Gross, was of Crostwick, in the same county. (Ibid. xi. 10.)

NO. XXV.—PEDANTRY AND PUNS.

Dr. Collins and Dr. Field, being to dispute before King James, had promised one another to lay aside all extravagancie of witt, and to buckle to a serious argumentation; but they soone violated their owne lawe, for Field beganne thus: " Sic disputas, Colendissime Collins," and Collins againe to him afterward, " Sic disputas, Ager Colende."

L'Estrange, No. 82. Mr. Greene.

The superlatives of this anecdote were evidently formed in the same school as one which created much merriment on King James's visit to Cambridge in 1614-15 ; when the University Orator, Sir Francis Nethersole, on complimenting the Prince of Wales, addressed him as *Jacobissime Carole;* " and some (adds Mr. Chamberlain) will needs add, that he called him *Jacobule* too ; which neither pleased the King nor any body else." Bishop Corbet, in his " Grave Poem " written on this occasion, thus versified the Orator's exordium :

> " I wonder what your Grace doth here,
> Who have expected been twelve yeare ;
> And this your son fair *Carolus,*
> That is so *Jacobissimus.*"   *(Progr. of James I. ii. 59, 69.)*

Dr. Richard Field, Prebendary of Windsor and Dean of Gloucester, who wrote, " Of the Church, Four Books," (Lond. 1606, fol.) was at one time, says Anthony Wood, "esteemed one of the best disputants in Oxon ; and so eminently the best that most scholars did acknowledge him to be so." In 1598 he was made Chaplain, and afterwards Chaplain in Ordinary to Queen Elizabeth ; and in the beginning of King James's reign received the same appointments to that Sovereign, and by his Majesty's own appointment, was sent for to be at Hampton Court. In 1604 he became Canon of Windsor, and in 1609 Dean of Gloucester. When King James I. heard him preach for the first time, he said, " This is a *Field* for God to dwell in," an expression, remarks Wood, not much unlike to that in the book called " The Holy War," where, in lib. iv. cap. 5, the author (Thomas Fuller), citing something out of the third book of *The Church,* written by our author Field, he stileth him, " that learned divine, whose memory smelleth like a field the Lord hath blessed." This worthy man, who was one of the first Fellows nominated by King James I. for the intended foundation of Chelsea College, died 15 Nov. 1616. (See Wood's Athenæ Oxon. ii. 183, ed. Bliss.)

Dr. Field was a disputant before the King at Oxford in 1605 (Nichols's Progresses, &c. of King James I. i. 533) ; but there was no Dr. Collins engaged in the disputation. In 1612-13, Mr. Samuel Collins (afterwards Regius Professor of Divinity and Provost of King's), was a disputant before Prince Charles *at Cambridge.* (Ibid. iii. 1086.) Both these learned men, therefore, though they were members of different Universities, were eminent in these scholastic exercises ; which is perhaps a sufficient foundation for this story. The latter will be noticed more fully hereafter under No. LXXI.

NO. XXVI.—TAKING AND MIS-TAKING.

A plaine country fellow overheard some gentlemen talking of for-raigne newes, and amongst other passages, one sayde it was most certainly reported that the King of Sweden was fallen into Bavaria, and had there taken Ratisbone (commonly called Reinsburgh, seated upon the Danaw), which fagge end of newes he greedily snatched away with him homeward, and tells his neighbours that he heard of a very lamentable accident to-day. "What is it?" said they. "Oh," sayes he, "who would ever have thought it, that brave fighting fellow the King of Sweden hath poisoned himselfe with taking of Ratsbane."

L'Estrange, No. 87. S. L.

"That brave fighting fellow," Gustavus Adolphus, who in his German campaigns, 1630-2, took every thing that came before him, was about the last man in the world to take "ratsbane in his porridge," &c. He died the death of a hero, "with his sword in his hand, the word of command in his mouth, and victory in his imagination," at the fatal battle of Lutzen, 6th November 1632; and which he had commenced by vociferating at the head of his army, Luther's celebrated version of the 46th Psalm, "*Ein feste burg ist ünser Gott,*" and by giving as the word of the day, "God be with us!"

NO. XXVII.—A GOOD EXPOSITION.

The Archbishop of Canterbury had an house by Croydon, pleasantly sited, but that it was too much wood-bound, so he cutt downe all upon the front to the high way. Not long after the Lord Chancellor Bacon riding by that way, ask't his man whose faire house that was. He told him, "My Lord of Canterburie's." "It is not possible," sayes he, for his building is environed with woode." "'Tis true, Sir," sayes he, "it was so, but he hath lately cut most of it downe." "By my troth," answered Bacon, "he has done very judiciously, for before me-thought it was a very obscure and darke place, but now he has expounded and cleared it up wonderfully well." *L'Estrange, No. 90. Dr. Stubbe.*

In Aubrey's Lives, ii. 225, this story is told "with a difference" of person and place.
"The Bishop of London did cutt down a noble clowd of trees at Fulham; the Lord Chancellor [Bacon] told him, he was a good expounder of darke places!"

NO. XXVIII.—OMNIA VANITAS.

Old Burleigh the Treasurer, hearing much fame of a gentleman's house in Suffolke, for the rarities to be seene there, went to visit him, and had presented to his view varietie of pretious gemmes, meddalls, birds, a wedge of Ophir gold (which certainly was an imposture, for the gentleman was but shallow and credulous, and easy to be deluded, for he had payde dear for many sophisticated things), choice of pictures, statues, and every roome embroidered with mottoes and devises; but at last he brought Burleigh into a roome where he would shew him a piece of infinite valew for the antiquitie, and that was Solomon's statue, cap-a-pie, cut while he lived (but it appear'd plainly to be an old weather-beaten statue of some ancient Philosopher), and his owne motto under, but thus written: " OMNIA VANITAS; " which when the Treasurer observed in so different a character, and purposing to put a grave slye squibbe upon him. " Sir," says he, " this does not well; I would advise you to alter by any meanes; for methinkes OMNIA is very little and VANITAS exceeding greate." " My Lord," sayes the gentleman (not apprehending the acute dilemma of his speech), " it shall be done; for to speake truly, *Vanitas* hath beene thus here a long time, and I crowded in *Omnia,* but I'le have my painter make them all one before your Lordshippe comes againe."

L'Estrange, No. 119. *My L. Cooke.*

Another version of this story may be found, where it was scarcely to be looked for, in the private correspondence of the American philosopher, Benjamin Franklin, who writing to Mrs. Bache, respecting a proposed order of American knighthood, and commenting upon a suggested motto, adds, "Every thing makes me recollect some story. A gentleman had built a very fine house, and thereby much impaired his fortune. He had a pride, however, in showing it to his acquaintance. One of them, after viewing it all, remarked a motto over the door, ŌIA VANITAS. ' What,' says he, ' is the meaning of this ŌIA, 'tis a word I don't understand.' ' I will tell you,' said the gentleman, ' I had a mind to have the motto cut on a piece of smooth marble; but there was not room for it between the ornaments to be put in characters large enough to be read; I therefore made use of a contraction, anciently very common in Latin manuscripts, whereby the *m*'s and *n*'s in words are omitted, and the omission noted by a little dash above, which you may see there, so that the word is *omnia*, OMNIA VANITAS.' ' O,' said his friend, ' I comprehend the meaning of your motto, it relates to your edifice ; and signifies, that if you have abridged your *omnia*, you have nevertheless left your VANITAS legible at full length.' '' (Priv. Corresp. of Franklin, I. 136.)

Franklin, it will be observed, could tell a plain tale with a simplicity truly republican ; but the concealed racy wit of '' old Burleigh, the Treasurer,'' was either beyond his grasp, or had escaped from his memory.

NO. XXIX.—QUEEN ELIZABETH'S KINDRED.

One begg'd of Queene Elizabeth, and pretended kindred and alliance, but there was no such relation. '' Friend,'' says she, '' grant it be so, do'st thinke I am bound to keepe all my kindred ? Why that's the way to make *me* a beggar.''   *L'Estrange, No.* 124. *Mr. Derham.*

This reply, full of good, shrewd, common sense, will match very fairly with that of the nobleman, who being importuned for assistance by one who claimed relationship, and upon being pressed to prove it, alleged their mutual descent from Adam, gave him a penny, saying, '' If all your relations do the same, you will be richer than I am ! ''

Queen Elizabeth had numerous maternal relations, and many of them among the inferior gentry (particularly in Norfolk), an inconvenience which arose from her father having selected for his second consort a subject of no very elevated extraction, whilst the blood of the Boleynes was widely diffused by the intermarriages of numerous junior branches. It is no doubt an historical truth, that the Queen chose to repress such claims of kindred ; and so sparing was she of her honours at all times, that her cousin-german Lord Hunsdon was never advanced above the rank of a Baron, whilst his brother-in-law Sir Francis Knollys was not even a peer, but only a Knight of the Garter. King Charles the First made the son of the latter Earl of Banbury ; and the grandson of the former Earl of Dover. Elizabeth made Sir Thomas Sackville, one of her second cousins, a Baron by the title of Lord Buckhurst ; yet, though his talents as a statesman afterwards raised him to the high office of Lord Treasurer, upon the death of Burleigh, he could not obtain the dignity of Earl until the first year of James, when he was made Earl of Dorset.

NO. XXX.—LORD COOKE'S SHOP.

A plaine country fellow comming to the Temple for councell in some point of Law, enquir'd for my Lord Cooke's shoppe.

L'Estrange, No. 133. *Thos. Bezome.*

Somewhat analogous to this definition of the Temple in the reign of James, is that which was bestowed upon the King's Bench, when Abbot Lord Tenterden was the Lord Chief Justice, namely, '' Abbot's Priory.''

NO. XXXI.—A CUT-PURSE CUT.

A gentleman at a play sate by a fellow that he strongly suspected for a cutt-purse, and, for the probation of him, took occasion to drawe out his purse and put it up so carelessly, as it dangled downe (but his eye watcht it strictly with a glance), and he bent his discourse another way; which his suspected neighbour observing, upon his first faire opportunitie, exercised his craft, and having gott his booty beganne to remove away, which the gentleman noting, instantly drawes his knife, and whipps off one of his eares, and vow'd he would have something for his mony. The Cutt-purse beganne to sweare and stampe, and threaten. " Nay, go to, Sirrah," sayes the other, " be quiete; I'le offer you faire, give me my purse againe, here 's your eare, take it, and be gone."

L'Estrange, No. 143. *My Cosin John Spelman.*

The cut-purses of James's time correspond with the pickpockets of the present day ; and James's first act of arbitrary power (probably also his least unpopular one, for it was highly commended at the time), was his summary suspension of a cut-purse at Newark, on his first progress into England. One of the most celebrated of these confounders of "meum et tuum " was Mary Frith, alias Moll Cut-purse, whose adventures form the subject of Middleton and Decker's play of the " Roaring Girl." Moll robbed General Fairfax on Hounslow Heath ; and at her death in 1659, left twenty pounds by will for the conduits to run with wine when King Charles the Second returned. (See Collier's Old Plays, vi. 1.)

NO. XXXII.—A BORN JUSTICE.

There was one Mr. Guybon, a gentleman of very weake understanding, but yet in Commission, who having often publish't his folly upon the Bench, at last sayes a sly plaine fellow to another, " I pray, Sir, was not Mr. Guybon borne a Justice of Peace ? " as, if his office had not descended upon him with his estate by right of inheritance, sure no man would ever have made him one.

L'Estrange, No. 145. *My Father.*

The Guybons are a well known Norfolk family, and the character given to the worthy justice is such as to render it not only unnecessary, but uncivil, to particularize him. Sir

Thomas Guybon, Knt. had by Agnes his second wife, daughter of Walter Baspole, of Norfolk, Gent. William Guybon, of Watlington, Gent. who married Elizabeth, daughter of Thomas
Drury, Gent. of Fincham, and left a son and heir, Sir Thomas Guybon, Knt. lord of the
manor of Thursford, who died in 1666, and was succeeded by his third and only surviving son
Francis, afterwards a Knight. (See Blomefield's Norfolk, v. 223.)

NO. XXXIII.—A MAN OF METAL.

Sir Richard Bingham was a man eminent both for spiritt and martiall
knowledge, but of a very small stature; and, understanding that a proper bigg-bon'd gentleman had traduc'd his little person, or Corpusculum,
with the ignominious tearme of Dande-pratt: "Tell him from mee,"
says he, "that, when it comes to the tutch, he shall find there is as
good silver in a Dande-pratt (which is a very small kind of coine) as in
a brodd-fac't groate."   *L'Estrange, No. 154. My Mother.*

This eminent commander, who has here anticipated Burns's idea:

> "The rank is but the guinea's stamp,
> A man's the gold for a' that."

was the second son of Thomas Bingham, Esq. of Bingham-Melcombe, in the county of
Dorset, by Alice daughter of Thomas Croker, esq. the ancestor of the present Earl of Lucan
and of Baron Clanmorris. He was one of the most celebrated Captains of the age in which
he lived, being at the time of the Spanish Armada one of Queen Elizabeth's Military Coun-
sel, and afterwards, for his valuable services in Ireland, constituted Marshall of that kingdom
and General of Leinster.

Camden, in his Remains, p. 188 (1637), tells us: "King Henry the Seventh stamped a
small coine called Dandy Prats;" and the name Dandiprat is also commonly applied to any
dwarf or little person; and Leake, in his "Historical Account of English Money," p. 270,
speaking of the state of the coinage at the close of the reign of Elizabeth, says, "that besides
the Queen's adulterate coin they had, *First*, broad-faced groats, coined originally for four-
pence, but now worth eighteenpence,' &c. These '*broad-faced groats*' are obviously those, on
which ' the bluff visage' of Harry the Eighth appears in all its breadth.

NO. XXXIV.—MIGHT MAKES RIGHT.

Sir Arthur Heveningham being inform'd of some abuse of his liber-
ties by a sawcy insolent fellow, he vow'd and threatned such a kind
of punishment presently as was not very legall; whereupon a friend of

his prompted him of the danger of such unwarrantable proceeding, as the letter of the law would not beare. " Oh pox on 't ! " sayes he, " in cases of this nature we must not be so nice and scrupulous ; lett's doe something by law and something by presumption."

L'Estrange, No. 159. Unc. Ri. Catline.

Sir Arthur Heveningham of Heveningham, Knt. was the eldest son of Sir Anthony Heveningham, by Mary daughter of John Shelton.

NO. XXXV.—A SPECIAL ENTAIL.

The Lord Chief Justice Richardson went with Mr. Mewtis, the Clarke of the Councell, to see his fine house at Gunnoss-bury, which was furnish't with many pretty knacks and rarities. My Lord view'd all, and lik't well, but, " Mr. Mewtis," sayes he, " if you and I agree upon the price, I must have all your fooleries and bables into the bargaine." " Why, my Lord," sayes he, " for those I will not stand with you. They may e'ene be entail'd, if you please, upon you and your heires."

L'Estrange, No. 160. Sir Rob. Bell.

Gunnersbury, in the parish of Ealing, co. Middlesex (in latter times the residence of the " old Princess Amelia," and now of the Baroness de Rothschild), appears to have frequently changed its occupiers ; but Lysons does not mention among them either Mr. Meautys or Chief Justice Richardson.

Mr. Meautys lives in remembrance as the faithful Secretary of Lord Bacon, who adhered to him throughout his misfortunes ; and, after his death, erected that monument in Saint Michael's Church, near Saint Alban's, which gives us the only image of the person of the great philosopher. Meautys (who had married Bacon's niece, and had succeeded him in the mansion at Gorhambury) himself lies unsculptured but not forgotten at his master's feet. The late Bishop Jebb, in a note to his edition of Burnet's Lives, p. 104, beautifully remarks : " Few and faint are the inscriptive characters which can now be traced of the modest Secretary's name ; but it is deeply engraven on many a kind and congenial heart. He who now guides the pen, once visited the church of Saint Michael, within the precincts of Old Verulam. He trusts he did so with no irreverent emotion ; and while he read the thrilling SIC SEDEBAT, he thought upon the faithful servant, who never viewed him so seated but with affectionate veneration." Mr. B. Montagu (Bacon's Works, vol. XVI. p. ccccxlix.) adds the result of some inquiries of his own respecting the grave of Meautys, made in 1829. One half of the simple inscription —

HERE LIETH THE BODY OF S^r
THOMAS MEAWTYS, K^t.

was then covered by a pew, and much of the other half was illegible. The pew has no doubt been removed, and the inscription repaired. A memorial so interesting ought never either to be defaced or hidden.

Some particulars of Sir Thomas Richardson will be found in the note to No. XCIII.

NO. XXXVI.—BOWLING IMPROVED.

My Lord Brookes us'd to be much resorted to by those of the preciser sort, who had got a powerful hand over him; yet they would allow him Christian libertie for his recreations : but being at bowles one day, in much company, and following his cast with much eagernesse, he cryed, " Rubbe, rubbe, rubbe, rubbe, rubbe." His chaplaine (a very strict mann) runns presently to him; and in the hearing of diverse, " O good my Lord, leave that to God—you must leave that to God !" sayes he.

L'Estrange, No. 164. *Mr. Russell.*

The nobleman, whose chaplain thus *improved*, as it is called, the Game at Bowls, was Robert Lord Brooke, who was killed at the storming of Lichfield in 1643, and of whom the Puritans believed that he was removed to Heaven, and the Royalists, however doubtful upon that point, that at least his death was a direct interposition of Providence.—(See Granger, ii. 144, ed. 1779.)

Strutt, in his Sports and Pastimes, book iii. c. vii. traces the game of bowls back to the thirteenth century and exhibits a view of three parties engaged in the pastime, from a beauful MS. Book of Players belonging to Mr. Douce. They are playing with a small bowl or jack, according to the modern practice.—(See p. 92 ; p. 267 of the 8vo edition.)

From a passage in Pepys's Diary, i. 289, in which he speaks of seeing " White Hall Garden and the Bowling Alley, where lords and ladies are now at bowles in fine condition," it will be seen that this game was played by both sexes, a fact which certainly has escaped Strutt's notice.

NO. XXXVII.—GREAT WITS JUMP.

Dr. Cougham was Dr. Franklin's pupill when he was of Christ's Colledge, and of intimate acquaintance with Mr. Power, whose note booke he stole one day out of his closett, and after preach't some of his sermons, which when it came to Power's eare, " Alas poore Asse," sayes he, " he is faine to live upon my provander." At last Dr. Franklyn charg'd Cougham with it, and rebukt him for an impudent plagiarie, and for robbing Power's hive so like a drone: " Why, Tutor," sayes he, " what I preach is mine owne, but it cannot be avoided but that sometimes we shall handle the same points, for you know good witts will jumpe." " By my troth, Cougham," says he, " that may very well be, for I have known thee *for a leaper* a long time ; " for he was seldome without some loathsome disease.

L'Estrange, No. 166. *Mr. Loades.*

William Power, B. D. was Fellow of Christ's College, Cambridge, and Lady Margaret's Professor. He was ejected from his Fellowship early in the rebellion, but retained his professorship until 1646.—(Vide Walker's Sufferings of the Clergy, pt. ii. 143.)

NO. XXXVIII.—A *DEEP-RED* DIVINE.

Upon high Festivalls the Bishoppe or Deane use to preach at Christ Church in Norwich, and to goe up into the pulpitt in their scarlett robes. On Christmas day it was the Deane's course, who preach't in his redde robes, and a poore silly woman being ask't when she came home who preach't at Christ Church ? " Truly," sayes she, " I knowe not; unless 't were one of our Aldermen, for I am sure he had a redd gowne." *L'Estrange, No.* 169. *My Coz. Dol. Gurney.*

NO. XXXIX.—WOLF'S COLLEGE, CAMBRIDGE.

Parson Noke, who never was of any universitie, was once interrogated by John Cremer, what colledge he was of in Cambridge : he, sensible of the squibbe, thought to stabbe him with his owne question, and would needs know what colledge he was of : " Who, I ? Mr. Noke," sayes he ; " why, of Wolfe's Colledge" (meaning the Rose Taverne). " Were you so ?" sayes he ; " you may e'en thank your good friends that were able to preferre you and doe so well by you."

L'Estrange, No. 174. *Mr. Loades.*

John Cremer, we presume, to be John Cremer, of Ingaldsthorpe, mentioned hereafter, No. 54; and the College in which he took his degree, was doubtless at that time one of the most frequented in the University. Pepys, in his Memoirs, iii. 375, says, " Thence away to Cambridge, and did take up at the Rose."

NO. XL.—AN AID TO DEVOTION.

A good, formall, precise Minister in the Isle of Wight us't to say that a glasse or two of wine extraordinarie would make a man praise God with much alacritie.   *L'Estrange, No. 175. My Wife.*

NO. XLI.—" SING OLD ROSE."

Rose the old Viole-maker, had a singular facultie in making sweete instruments for single play, and, amongst other musical discourses, one was saying he knew where there was a very choice Rose Viole, and he did not think but it was at least thirty yeare old. John Holman, being by, " I protest," sayes he, " my father has an excellent good Viole, I doe not think but it will be a Rosse within these two yeare, for I am sure 't is eight and twentie yeare old." ·

L'Estrange, No. 179. My Bro. Roger.

Whether Rose, alias Rosse, " the Old Viol Maker," be at all connected with ' Old Rose,' whose name is immortalized in the Song mentioned by honest Isaak Walton (and printed in the Gentleman's Magazine for August 1829, p. 111), it is for wiser antiquaries to determine. Thus much, however, is certain, that he was the son of John Rose, citizen of London, living in Bridewell, and who is said by Stowe, in his Annals (p. 869), to have invented a species of lute which he called the Bandore in the fourth year of Queen Elizabeth.—See Hawkins's History of Music, iii. 345, n.; and further, iv. 339, n.; where he quotes from a Collection of Airs, entitled, " Triple Concordia," published by John Carr, living at the Middle Temple Gate in Fleet Street, the following advertisement, and tells us that the John Ross there spoken of, is the son of the John Rose beforementioned:

" There is two Chests of Viols to be sold, one made by Mr. John Ross, who formerly lived in Bridewell, containing two trebles, three tenors, and one basse; the chest was made in the year 1598. The other being made by Mr. Henry Smith, who formerly lived over against Hatton-house in Holbourn, containing two trebles, two tenors, two basses. The chest was made in the year 1633. Both chests are very curious work."

NO. XLII.—NEVER BRANDED BEFORE.

A rogue was branded on the hand, and before he went from the barre, the Judge bad them search if he were not branded before. " No, my Lord, I was never branded *before.*" They search't and found the marke. " Oh you 're an impudent slave, what thinke you now ? " " I cry your Honor mercy," sayes he, " for I ever thought my shoulders stood behind." *L'Estrange, No.* 183. *Anonymous.*

NO. XLIII.—HEARING VERSUS UNDERSTANDING.

Sir Julius Cæsar, Master of the Rolls, was reputed none of the deepest men, and had many slye jerks passed upon him ; amongst others, he was once hearing of a cause somewhat too intricate for his capacitie, and his judgment beganne to incline the wrong way. The Court at that time being very lowde and clamorous, one of Councell to the ad- verse part, stepps up and calls out, " Silence there, my masters : yee keepe such a bawling the Master of the Rolls cannot *understand* a word that 's spoken."

L'Estrange, No. 195. *Mr. Spring.*

No one ought to think of this " slye jerk," without at the same time calling to mind, that which was a counterpoise for many failings, Sir Julius Cæsar's boundless benevolence and philanthropy. His coach was as well known to the poor as any hospital in England ; and a gentleman who borrowed it, was so beset by Sir Julius's poor pensioners, that it cost him more than would have hired twenty coaches to satisfy their importunity. This excellent man shared with Meautys the glory of adhering to Bacon through all his troubles. The philoso- pher wrote some of his greatest works in Cæsar's house, drew in his distresses upon Cæsar's bounty, and, finally, died in his arms.—(Vide Lloyd's State Worthies, 934 ; Bacon's Works by Montagu, xvi. cccxxiv.)

NO. XLIV.—PRINTING AND PAINTING.

Sir John Heydon and the Lady Cary had good witts, and lov'd to be breaking of staves one upon another. Sir John comes in one day very briske, in a payre of printed velvett breeches (which was then the fashion), but some way defective, so as she had a flurt at them presently. " Hold you contented, good Madame," sayes he ; " for if it were not for Printing and Painting, your face and my breech would soone be out of fashion." *L'Estrange, No.* 200. *My Father.*

Sir John Heydon, second son of Sir Christopher Heydon, of Baconsthorp, co. Norfolk. He was knighted in Aug. 1620, and succeeded his brother Sir William at Baconsthorp in 1627. He was Lieutenant-general of the Ordnance to Charles the First during the Civil War ; and his being created D.C.L. at Oxford, Dec. 20, 1642, gives occasion to Wood to say : " He was as great scholar as a soldier, especially in the mathematics ; suffered much for his Majesty's cause ; and died 16 Oct. an. 1653."—(Wood's Fasti Oxon. edit. by Bliss, ii. 43.)

Lady Cary (of whom we shall have occasion to speak when we come to No. 124), like the fair Ophelia, not content with the face given to her, had by painting " given herself another ; " a practice now fast falling into disuse, but which prevailed when these anecdotes were penned to a most extraordinary degree. Her ladyship's appointment of " Mistress of the Sweet Coffers " to Anne of Denmark, might probably have required a peculiar knowledge of *cosmetics*, which she appears to have been willing to learn by experience.

NO. XLV.—THE METAL THE COMMANDMENTS ARE MADE OF.

Young Sir Drue Drury call'd for tobacco-pipes at a taverne ; the fellow bringes some, and in laying them downe upon the table, most of them brake ; he sware a great oathe presently that they were made of the same mettall with the Commandements : " Why so ? " sayes one. " Why, because they are so soone broken."

L'Estrange, No. 201. *Mr. Spring.*

" Young Sir Drue Drury " (already mentioned in No. 1,) was either the knight of that name, who was son of Sir Drue Drury, of Linsted in Kent, the Gentleman Usher of the Privy Chamber to Queen Elizabeth, and which young Sir Drue was created a Baronet in May 1627, and died in 1632 ; or else a younger Sir Drue, namely the second Baronet of the name, and who was born in 1611.

NO. XLVI.—AN OUT OF THE WAY REPROOF.

King James, being hunting in the North, was forc't out of the field by a tempest, and a church being the nearest building, there he takes sanctuarie, and thrusts into an obscure and low seate, being very meanly habited and attended. The minister had newly stept into the pulpitt, and spyed some beames of his Majestie through all those cloudes, but tooke no farther notice on 't. He falls to his worke, dicotomizeth his text, and proceeds a little way very logically with the parts : at last he suddenly digresses cleane from the point, and falls into a bitter declamation against swearing, and runns out all his sand upon that subject. The Sermon ended, the King sends for him to dinner, and when they were merry, " Parson," sayes he, " why didst thou flee so from thy text?" " If it please your Majestie," sayes he, " when you tooke the paines to come so far out of your way to heare me, I thought it very good manners for me to steppe a little out of my text to meete with your Majestie." " By my saul, mon," sayes the King, " and thou hast mette with me so as never mon did! "

L'Estrange, No. 202. Sir W. Spring.

This anecdote furnishes us with two of the most strongly marked peculiarities of James's character, his fondness for hunting and his habit of swearing. " I dare boldly say," says Osborne, in his Memoirs, " that one man in his reign might with more safety have killed another than a rascal deer ; but if a stag had known to have miscarried, and the author fled, a proclamation, with a description of the party, had been presently penned by the Attorney-general, and the penalty of his Majesty's high displeasure (by which was understood the Star Chamber), threatened against all that did abet, comfort, or relieve him ; thus satyrical, or if you please tragical, was this sylvan prince against deer-killers, and indulgent to man-slayers."

While Dalyell, in his " Sketches of Scottish History," p. 86, tells us, " He would make a great deal too bold with God in his passion, both with cursing and swearing, and a strain higher verging on blasphemy ; but would, in his better temper say, ' he hoped God would not impute them as sins, and lay them to his charge, seeing they proceeded from passion. He had need of great assistance rather than hope, that would make thus bold with God.' "

NO. XLVII.—A FOX DRAWS AN INFERENCE AND CARRIES A PIG.

To proove that the creature hath a kind of reasoning with itselfe, Sir Henry Wotton told this story to King James (who was credulous enough in that point). A fox had killed a little pigge, and was to passe a river to his denne ; by the water side alders had been newly stubb'd, and there lay chipps of all sizes; the foxe before he would venter himselfe and his prey into the streame, weighs the danger, weighs his pigge, and weighs diverse chipps after it: at last he takes up into his mouth one of the heaviest, passeth the river with it, and arriving safely, comes backe and fetches over his pigge.

L'Estrange, No. 203. Sir W. Spring.

Though James is here represented as " credulous enough," Sir Henry Wotton related this anecdote (perhaps derived from dear old Isaak Walton) not as a trial of his credulity, but as contributing to that knowledge which gained for him the title of the British Solomon, a title by which he was commonly called among his courtiers. In a story in the present collection, curiously illustrative of James's personal dirtiness, but, which like too many others, is far too filthy to be drawn from its present obscurity, we find Ramsay Lord Holdernesse addressing the Royal attendants in James's presence, " My Lords, see our Salaman! Is this the Salaman you talke on? If ever old Salaman, in all his royaltie, was *a Rayde* like ours, I 'le be hanged!"

" Great Britain's Solomon!" is the title of the Sermon preachéd by John Bishop of Lincoln at James's funeral on the 7th May 1625. The text is taken from 1 Kings, c. xi. v. 41, " And the rest of the acts of Solomon, and all that he did, and his wisdom, are they not written in the book of the acts of Solomon;" 42. "And the time that Solomon reigned in Jerusalem over all Israel was forty years;" 43. " And Solomon slept with his fathers, and was buried in the city of David his father; and Rehoboam his son reigned in his stead."

The Sermon consists in a great measure of a parallel between Solomon and James, and contains the following passage, which is curious for its allusion to Charles's attendance as chief mourner, and to the effigy of the deceased monarch in the hearse or catafalco (which is represented in the plate prefixed to the Sermon, and copied in Nichols's Progresses, &c. vol. iv.):

" For God hath provided another statue yet to adorne the exequies of our late Soveraigne. I doe not meane this artificial representation within the hearse, for this shows no more than his outward bodie, or rather the bodie of his bodie, his cloathes and ornaments; but I meane that statue which (beyond all former præsidents of pietie) walkt on foote this day after the hearse, one of Myron's statues—

" Qui pene hominū animas effinxerit;

" Which came so neare to the soules of men, a breathing statue of all his vertues. This God hath done for him, or rather for us; for as he hath made a lively representation of the vertues of Solomon in the person of King James, so hath he done a like representation of the vertues of King James in the person of King Charles our gracious Sovereign."

NO. XLVIII.—A FOX PLAYS A FOWL TRICK.

The fellow to this did the Earle of Southampton relate to King James. In his Hawking Brooke at Shellingford, he saw diverse fowle upon the river, and a little way up the streame a Foxe very busie by the banke-side. He delay'd his sporte, on purpose to see what that creature would doe. The Foxe stepps by and sheeres up sometimes a scare brake, sometimes a greene weede, puts them into the water and so letts them drive downe upon the Fowle; after he had well embold'ned them by this stratagem, he putts many in together, and himselfe after them with one in his mouth; and under this covert, gaining upon the thickest part of the fowle, suddenly darts from his ambush and catches one. This did the Earl report as an eye-witnesse.

L'Estrange, No. 204. Sir W. Spring.

The Earl of Southampton was Henry Wriothesley, the friend of Shakspeare, and to whom Dr. Drake, in his Shakspeare and his Times, supposes the Sonnets to have been dedicated. It has, however, been since ascertained, by the investigations of the late Mr. Boaden and of B. Heywood Bright, Esq. (see the Gentleman's Magazine for 1832, pt. ii. pp. 296, 407), and more recently by those of Mr. Armitage Brown, in his interesting volume, "Shakspeare's Autobiographical Poems," that "Mr. W. H. the Begetter of these Sonnets," was William Herbert, afterwards Earl of Pembroke. Tieck, the German Poet, whose knowledge and appreciation of our early dramatic poetry have rarely been excelled, published a very interesting Essay on Shakspeare's Sonnets in the German Taschenbuch "Penelope" for 1826, in which he treats them as containing the real materials for a life of the Poet; and as having been addressed to his friend and patron the Earl of Southampton.

To return, however, to the story related by Lord Southampton, we may observe, that in Lord Brougham's lately published "Dissertations on Subjects of Science connected with Natural Theology," his lordship, in treating on "Instinct," relates an anecdote of a fox very similar to the present one :—"The cunning of foxes is proverbial; but I know not if it was ever more remarkably displayed than in the Duke of Beaufort's country, where Reynard, being hard pressed, disappeared suddenly, and was, after strict search, found immersed in a waterpool up to the very snout, by which he held a willow bough hanging over the pond."

NO. XLIX.—VICE VERSA.

Old Sir Nicholas Bacon, of Suffolke, upon some contest betwixt him and a scholler whose name was Pye: "Well, Mr. Pye," sayes he, "goe your wayes, I believe I shall sit upon your skirts for't:"—"That will be a rare thinge," sayes he; "Pye upon Hogge is common, but Hogge upon Pye did I never see." 　　　*L'Estrange, No. 215. Mr. Spring.*

Sir Nicholas Bacon was the eldest son of Sir Nicholas Bacon the Lord Keeper, and half-brother of the great Lord Bacon. He had been knighted by Elizabeth in 1578, and was the first person advanced to the dignity of a Baronet upon the institution of that order in 1611.

NO. L.—A TALE OF WIGGETT.

One was telling the tale of Wiggett, who ranne another foole off from the Castle Hill at Norwich, and as they tumbled cryde out, " Now Foole, now Barrow; now Foole, now Barrow;" and one Mr. Barrow sat by, who jealous of the speech, and observing many eyes upon him, " Nay, Sirs," says he, " *I* am the Barrow, the Foole must be found some-where else."   *L'Estrange, No. 216. Mr. Spring.*

The present Collection contains several other tales (viz. Nos. 14, 127, and 128), of Wiggett, " the famous Facetious Foole," as he is styled in one of them, which, though they serve to illustrate the manners of the times, are much too gross to be drawn from the manuscript in which they are at present concealed.

Wiggett, who was no doubt a member of the Norfolk family of that name, would seem from an act of indecent rudeness which he is reported to have been guilty of towards the judges at an assize dinner at Norwich, to have belonged to that class of professed jesters styled by Mr. Douce, in his Dissertation on the Clowns and Fools of Shakspeare (Illustrations, ii. 304), *the City or Corporation Fool*, whose office was to assist in public entertainments and in pageants; and of which division of the fool-ish brotherhood the Lord Mayor's Fool, who is proverbially said to have " liked every thing that is good," was no doubt a member. It is somewhat remarkable, that Flögel, who has devoted a whole volume (" Geschichte der Hof-narren,") to the history of fools of all sorts, though his title-page speaks only of Court Jesters, should have omitted to mention the Corporation Fool, while, in his " Geschichte der Komischen Litteratur," i. 329, he not only speaks of the " Spruchsprecher," who clearly belonged to this class, but gives a portrait of Wilhelm Weber, who filled that office at Nuremberg, doubtlessly with greater reputation than Wiggett at Norwich.

By-the-bye, Blomefield, in his " History of Norfolk," ii. 737, quotes an inventory of the goods of the ancient Company of Saint George at Norwich, in which mention is made of " two habits, one for the *club-bearer*, another for his man, who are now called fools;" it is, therefore, not too much to suppose, that Wiggett held one or other of these offices.

NO. LI.—ARION ON A DOLPHIN'S BACK.

There was a spectacle presented to Queen Elizabeth upon the water, and amongst others Harry Goldingham was to represent Arion upon the dolphin's backe, but finding his voice to be very hoarse and un-pleasant when he came to performe it, he teares of his disguise and sweares he was none of Arion not he, but eene honest Harry Golding-ham; which blunt discoverie pleas'd the Quene better than if it had gone through in the right way; yet he could order his voice to an in-strument exceeding well.   *L'Estrange, No. 221. Mr. Spring.*

Queen Elizabeth made a memorable progress into Norfolk in 1578; and the celebrated Thomas Churchyard, who was engaged to prepare for her Majesty's entertainment, says, in a tract which he published respecting it : " I was the fyrste that was called, and came to Nor-wiche aboute that businesse, and remayned there three long weekes before the Courte came thether, devising and studying the best I coulde for the Citie ; albeit other gentlemen, as *Maister Goldingham*, Maister Garter, and others, dyd steppe in after, and broughte to passe that alreadye is sette in print in a booke."   But Goldingham had before been similarly employed at Kenilworth in 1575 ; for Gascoigne, in his " Princely Pleasures of Kenelworth," says, " The verses, as I think, were penned, some by Master Hunnes, some by Master Fer-rers, and some by *Master Goldingham ;* " and it was there that the performance of Arion, alluded to in this anecdote, took place (see Nichols's Progresses of Queen Elizabeth, i. 458, 502).   Sir Walter Scott has made use of this anecdote in his Romance of Kenilworth ; in which Michael Lambourne figures as Arion.   It may be added, that there is a poem by Harry Goldingham, entitled, " The Garden Plot," remaining in manuscript in the MS. Harl. 6902, the dedication of which to the Queen is printed in the Progresses, ii. 135.

The following anecdote, from L'Estrange MS. illustrates the love of mischief for which Mas-ter Harry appears to have been distinguished : " Harry Goldingham had a very little wench to his wife, and a Lord coming through the towne, called at his house ; he and his wife came out, and the Lord offered to light to salute her. ' O pray spare your paines, my Lord,' sayes he, ' I'le give her you up ; you shall kisse her on horsebacke."   As soon as he had her, Harry Goldingham switches the horse on the breech ; away runns he, being a mettled nagge (for my Lord had no hands to hold him, unlesse he should have throwne away the woman, and broke her necke).   After him runs Goldingham amaine, crying out, ' Stoppe my Lord, stoppe my Lord, stoppe my Lord, there ; he runns away with my wife.' "

NO. LII.—HOW SACRIFICES SHOULD BE PERFORMED.

Ben: Johnson was at a taverne and in comes Bishoppe Corbett (but not so then) into the next roome ; Ben: Johnson calls for a quart of *raw* wine, gives it the tapster : " Sirrha," sayes he, " carry this to the gentleman in the next chamber, and tell him I *sac*rifice my service to

him;" the fellow did so, and in those words: " Friend," sayes Dr.
Corbett, " I thanke him for his love; but pr'y thee tell hym from me
hee's mistaken, for *sac*rifices are allwayes *burn't.*"

L'Estrange, No. 222. Mr. Spring.

This anecdote, illustrative of the love of good liquor in general, and *burnt sack* in particular, manifested by Bishop Corbet, is confirmed by Aubrey ; who, in his Lives (ii. 293),
after telling us, what we can readily believe, " that his conversation was extreme pleasant,"
adds, " His chaplaine, Dr. Lushington, was a very learned and ingeniose man, and they
loved one another. The Bishop sometimes would take the key of the wine cellar, and he
and his Chaplaine would goe, and lock themselves in and be merry. Then first he layes
downe his episcopal hat,—' There lyes the Dr.' Then he putts off his gowne, ' There lyes
the Bishop.' Then 'twas, ' Here's to thee, Corbet,' and ' Here's to thee, Lushington.' "

NO. LIII.—OFF WITH YOUR JERKIN.

Sir Thomas Jermin going out with his Brooke Hawkes one evening at
Burry, they were no sooner abroad but fowle were found. He calls
out to one of his Falconers : " Lett out your Jerkin; off with your
Jerkin." The fellow being into the wind did not heare him: he stormes
and cries out still,—" Off with your Jerkin, you knave, off with your
Jerkin ! " Now it fell out there was at that instant a plaine townsman
of Burry, in a freeze Jerkin, stood betwixt him and his Falconer, who
seeing Sir Thomas in such a rage, and thinking he had spoken to him,
unbuttons amaine, throwes off his Jerkin, and beseeches his worshippe
not to be offended, for he would off with his doublet too to give him
content.   *L'Estrange, No. 223. Mr. Spring.*

Some readers, in order to understand this anecdote, may require to be informed that
Jerkin was a colloquial abbreviation of *Gerfalcon.*

The Jermyns of Rushbrooke were an ancient Suffolk family. This Sir Thomas, who had
been created a Knight of the Bath at the Coronation of James I. in 1603, has been mentioned
in the note to No. xx. as one of the " Fools " of Lord Hay's French embassy, and an anecdote of his sporting practices will be found hereafter, No. LXXXI. He became Vice Chamberlain to Charles I. and a Privy Councillor. His second son was the Henry Jermyn created, in 1643, Lord Jermyn of St. Edmund's Bury, and, after the Restoration, Earl of Saint
Alban's, whose intimacy with Henrietta Maria occasioned much scandal ; a passage in Sir John
Reresby's Memoirs has been considered an authority for the belief that they were privately
married. Sir Thomas Jermyn died in January 1644, and was buried at Rushbrook.

NO. LIV.—LICENSE OF THE PULPIT.

Sir William Woddhowse and Sir Robert Drury were allwayes at deadly feude, and there was a parson that favour'd Sir Robert, and declaimed often against Sir William in the pulpitt. Sir William, one day, meetes this parson in a boate at London, and makes no more adoe but trices him up, and throwes him into the Thames. The parson, as soon as he comes downe into the country, falls upon his old way, and no sooner enters his text and divides, but digresseth presently into a most bitter invective against Sir William Woddhowse. At that time a man of Sir William's chanc't to be there, and satt very neere the pulpitt, who, impatient to heare his master so revil'd, and spying the parsone's sleeve hang downe, catches hold on 't, (when the parson was most eager, and on his tiptoes,) yerkes him out among his parishioners, and away he runnes. *L'Estrange, No. 224. Mr. Spring.*

This story will appear scarcely credible to those who are acquainted with only the pulpit-practises of modern times; the readers of Latimer will perhaps give some little credence to it, and an anecdote, which exists upon the grave authority of "The State Trials," will tend towards the conversion of some others of my readers. In "The Book of Martyrs" there is a story of one Greenwood, of Suffolk, who was said to have perjured himself, in Queen Mary's time, in some case of heresy before the Bishop of Norwich; Fox adds, that afterwards, by the just judgment of Providence, his bowels rotted within him and he died. One Prest, a clergyman in Elizabeth's reign, happened to be presented to the living of the parish in which Greenwood was thought to have lived, and in one of his first discourses he selected Greenwood's history as a topic of discourse, and urged home upon his parishioners many deductions from it, respecting the sin of perjury. It so happened that Greenwood was in the church, and heard the discourse, but, probably, being a more phlegmatic person than Sir William Wodehouse's man, he replied not in person but by attorney. He brought his action against the clergyman for a libel, and the cause was tried, but without producing any satisfaction to Greenwood, for the Lord Chief Justice Wray, who tried it, directed the jury to find for the defendant, for that it appeared it was not done out of malice.—(State Trials, vol. xiii. p. 1387.)

NO. LV.—A DRY DUTCHMAN.

John Cremer, of Inglesthorpe, was at a taverne with Mr. Hasdoncke (a German), a temperate sober man, who had the patent for Inning the

Salt Marshes. " Sir," sayes John Cremer to him, " I doe not thinke you are a right Dutchman." " Why so ? " sayes he. " Because you will not drinke," sayes Cremer. " I pray what doe you take me to be, then ? " says Hasdoncke. " Why for a Jew," sayes Cremer, " because you take away our land and give us nothing for it : " for indeed he was. reduc'd but to an hard composition himselfe.

L'Estrange, No. 266. My Father.

John Cremer, of Ingaldesthorp, gent. died on 12th Jan. 1652, aged 70. See his epitaph in Hist. of Norfolk, edit. 1807, x. 338.

NO. LVI.—HONESTY REWARDED.

A gentleman overtakes in the evening a plaine country fellow, and ask't him how far it was to such a towne. " Tenne miles, Sir," sayes he. " It is not possible," sayes the gentleman. " It is no lesse," sayes the fellow. " I telle you it was never counted above five."— " 'Tis tenne indeed, Sir," sayes the fellow—and thus they were arguing *pro et con* a long time. At last sayes the countryman to him, " I'le tell you what I'le doe, Sir, because you seeme to be an honest gentleman, and your horse is almost tyr'd, I will not stand with you, you shall have it for five ; but, as I live, whosoever comes next shall ride tenne."

L'Estrange, No. 270. Bro. Spring.

NO. LVII.—AUT HEYLIN AUT DIABOLUS.

Reily, preaching upon this text, Job i. v. 7, it fortun'd that Heylin, of Oxford, who wrote a booke of Cosmography, and another about the Sabbath, was there as auditor : " Now," sayes Reily, upon the ana- lyzing his text, " if ye would know who it was that went thus to and fro, and compassed the earth, it was *that* Geographical Knave, the Devil

I meane." But few understood him so, for though his eye went another way, his finger was point blanke upon Heylin.

L'Estrange, No. 274. *Sir W. Spring.*

Reily probably belonged to the Puritans, amongst whom Heylin was exceedingly unpopular. His " Cosmography " involved him in some trouble with the Court, which is worthy of being alluded to on account of his reply. The offence taken was, that he had given precedency to the French King, and had styled France a more famous kingdom than England, at which James was so greatly irritated, that he ordered the Lord Keeper to suppress the book. Heylin, who was never over-scrupulous, declared that the first passage was entirely a mistake of the printer, who had put *is* instead of *was;* and that as to the second, when he mentioned the precedency of France before England, he did not allude to England, as it then stood augmented by Scotland, besides which he took what he did say from " Camden's Remains." His book " about the Sabbath " was written to reconcile the people to the " Book of Sports."

NO. LVIII.—A HOUSE FULL OF TOKENS.

The Earle of Arundell, Lord Marshall, had the sole patent for coining of new farthings, with a distinct marke for their currancy (because many were counterfeited before) ; and when he went Embassador to the Emperour the Mint house was well stor'd but lock't up untill his returne. The sicknesse being then in London, and poore people wanting their coine, some knave or other in the night, clap't a redde crosse upon the dore, and thus underwritt it : " Lord, have mercy upon us, for this house is full of tokens." *L'Estrange, No.* 281. *My Father.*

Thomas Howard, Earl of Arundel, Earl Marshal, here referred to, was the collector of the well-known Arundelian Marbles ; and it was on the occasion of this embassy to Vienna, which took place in 1636 (and of which an account was drawn up and published by Crowne, who attended his Lordship), that he found Hollar at Prague ; and brought him back with him to this country. An account of the new issue of Farthing Tokens, which was authorised by a Royal Proclamation in March 1635-6, will be found in Ruding's Annals of the Coinage, 1817, ii. 251. A small piece of brass let into the centre of the copper blanks from which they were struck, was the " distinct marke " by which they were authenticated.

The pun in the Londoner, alluding both to the coins and the signs of the plague, requires no illustration ; but it may not be out of place to suggest, whether the practice of marking a red cross upon the doors of infected houses might not have arisen from the injunction given to Moses at the institution of the passover; see Exodus, c. xii. v. 7, " And they shall take of the blood, and strike it on the two side posts, and on the upper door post of the houses wherein they dwell ;" v. 13. " And the blood shall be to you for a *token* upon the houses where ye are ; and when I see the blood I will pass over you, and the plague shall not be upon you to destroy you when I smite the land of Egypt."

Of the practice itself, we find the following account in Collier's Old Plays, xi. 544 :

" When a house became infected, the officers impowered for that purpose immediately placed a guard before it, which continued there night and day, to prevent any person going from thence, until the expiration of forty days. At the same time *red crosses of a foot long* were painted upon the doors and windows with the words, LORD HAVE MERCY UPON US ! in great letters written over them, to caution all passengers to avoid infected places."

NO. LIX.—ALTARING THE CHANCELS.

When they were so hott about Ceremonies, and removing the Communion Table out of the bodie of the Church, to place it Altar-wise in the Chancell; one ask't what newes from Cambridge : " Why," sayes he, " doe you not heare ? They are *Altaring* all their Chappells and Chancells there." *L'Estrange, No. 285. Mr. Hudson.*

Clarendon admirably describes the heats which are here referred to. " The expense of buying a new table, the inclosing it with a rail of joiner's work to fence it from the approach of dogs and all servile uses, the obliging all persons to come up to those rails to receive the sacrament, and the manner, gesture, and posture in the celebration of it, were the ingredients in the dispute, which was prosecuted " with the same earnestness and contention for victory as if the life of Christianity had been at stake."—(History of the Rebellion, i. 95.)

NO. LX.—THE OFFICE OF AN ATTORNEY-GENERAL.

Noy, who was the King's Atturney, and a busy projector, was check't a little in private by a friend for innovating and bearing too hard upon the poore subject. " O, but dost not thou know," sayes Noy, " that *Atturnatus* Domini Regis is one that must serve *the King's turne ?* " *L'Estrange, No. 296. My Father.*

Noy had need of all his wit to defend himself against the attacks made upon him on account of his change of party. He died before the schemes he devised, to replenish the Exchequer, were brought to bear; and great was the rejoicing everywhere except at Court. Wood says, that " the players .... the next terme after his decease, made him the subject of a merry comedy, styled, " *A Projector lately Dead, &c.*" What fate after death, or other meaning couched under the *&c.* in this title, I cannot tell. I have not been able to find any trace of such a play. (Wood's Athenæ, ii. 584, ed. Bliss.) Noy afforded a singular instance of what may be accomplished by the blandishments and flattery of a Court. His opposition had been of the sturdiest character; and it was only by dint of " great industry and importunity from Court, that he suffer'd himself to be made the King's Attorney General." The result is admirably told by Clarendon. " The Court made no impression upon his manners, upon his mind it did; and though he wore about him an affected morosity, which made him unapt to flatter other men, yet even that morosity and pride rendered him the most liable to be grossly flattered himself that can be imagined; and by this means, the great persons who steer'd the publick affairs, by admiring his parts and extolling his judgment, as well to his face as behind his back, wrought upon him by degrees for the eminency of the service, to be an instrument in all their designs."—(History of the Rebellion, vol. i. book 1.)

NO. LXI.—LAWYER WISE A WISE LAWYER.

Noy us'd to say of Wise, a lawyer of Lincolne's Inne (a very subtile and acute man in all businesse he undertooke), that he was like a mouse among joynt stooles; one may see where he moves and runnes, but no man knowes where to hitt himm.

L'Estrange, No. 297. My Father.

NO. LXII.—" HE COULD ON EITHER SIDE DISPUTE."

Dr. Love told Dr. Collins, " Nay, wee know well enough what you are (insinuating his Arminianisme); for you disputed both wayes." " Nay," sayes Collins, " for that very reason you don't know what I am." *L'Estrange, No. 298. Mr. Hudson.*

Richard Love, of Clare-hall, was one of the performers in Ignoramus when it was first acted before King James at Cambridge in 1614-15. (Progresses of King James, iii. 53.) He afterwards became Master of Corpus and Margaret Professor of Divinity; and surviving the Restoration, was selected to congratulate the King on his road to London on the part of the University. He was immediately made Dean of Ely; but died a few months after, in Jan. 1660-1. There is a particular memoir of him in Martin's History of Benet College; and of his portrait preserved in that house, there is an etching by Mr. Tyson.

Of Dr. Collins an account will be found in the note to No. LXXI.

NO. LXIII.—SANCTUARY.

When there was a feare of Invasion, some schollers in Cambridge were talking merrily how they would shift, and where they would hide themselves. " Well," sayes one (that was Bachelor of Divinitie, but never appeared in St. Marie's), " you have provided for yourselves, but nobody takes care of me." " Yes, 'faith," sayes another, " I'le hide thee where I'le warrant thou shalt nere be found." " Where 's that ? " sayes he. " Why in St. Marie's pulpitt," sayes the other; " The safest place for thee in the world, for ever any man lookes for thee there, I'll be hanged."   *L'Estrange, No.* 300. *Mr. Loades.*

NO. LXIV.—A LEAD MINE CURED OF THE DROPSY.

There was a Leade Mine in Derbishire, which yeelded infinite profitt, but that the waters rose so quicke as they would not worke but by ejection of it with engines. At last Sir Cornelius Vermuden he undertook it, but in another way, yet with very good successe; for he cutt a vault draine from a river up to it: upon which one sayd wittily, that " he had given his mother (the Earth) the best and most naturall physicke in the world; for that which others had allwayes attempted by violent and strong vomitts, he had now effected with a gentle purge."

L'Estrange, No. 303. *Mr. Derham.*

Sir Cornelius Vermuyden was a Zealander, whose first connection with this country was a project for draining the fens of Cambridgeshire in the reign of James I. This plan was not carried into effect ; but he afterwards was completely successful in draining the level of the royal chace of Hatfield, near Doncaster ; a very interesting account of which, and of the colony of his countrymen which he settled there, will be found in Hunter's History of the Deanery of Doncaster, vol. i. pp. 160 *et seq.* He was knighted by King Charles, Jan. 6, 1629. Subsequently, about the year 1631, he took a lease for thirty years of the Dove-gang lead mine, near Wirksworth, reckoned the best in Derbyshire, to which we may presume that the present anecdote relates.—(See the Gentleman's Magazine, vol. lxv. p. 300.)

It is melancholy to add, that this ingenious man at last " died miserably poor ;" but such was also the fate of his immediate predecessors John Trewe, the supposed inventor of canal locks (see the Archæologia, vol. xxviii), and of Sir Hugh Myddelton, the great metropolitan benefactor in that necessary article fresh water; and probably of other engineers, whose conceptions were more suited to this enterprising age of steam-carriages and viaducts than to their own.

NO. LXV.—MARRYING AND MARRING.

This proverbial saying passeth upon marriages: That a yong man and woman is a match of God's making,—so Adam and Eve; an old man and a yong woman of our Lady's,—so Joseph and Mary; but a yong man and an old woman of the divell's making.

L'Estrange, No. 304. *Mr. Derham.*

NO. LXVI.—GIVING LEG-BAIL.

One Jean Schwartz, a famous German painter, being to worke a roofe-piece in a publique and common towne hall, and to doe it by the day, grew very idle, so that the magistrates and overseers of the worke ever now and then were faine to hunt him out of the tavernes. Hee sees he could not drinke in quiet; against the next morning he stuffs a paire of stockings and shooes, sutable to those he wore, hangs them downe betwixt his staging where he satt to worke (for being overhead he did either sett, lye, or leane to it all), removes them a little once or twice a day, and takes them up at noone and night; and with this fallacy dranke without any disturbance a fortnight together (the hoste of the next taverne being privy to the plott, and his trusty friend), for the officers coming in once or twice a day to look after him, and seeing his leggs hang downe, suspected nothing, but extolled their convert Jean Swarts, and proclaimed him for the most laborious and conscionable painter in the world. *L'Estrange, No.* 309. *Mr. Stettkin.*

Pilkington tells us this facetious artist was born at Groningen in Holland, in 1480, and went for improvement to Italy. He painted History and Landscape equally well, the latter much in the manner of Schozel. He died in 1541.

The same J. Zwarts had admirably well perform'd the Historie of
our Saviour's Passion, in a large table, and in oyl'd colours; and a Cardinal was so taken with it, as he resolved to bring the Pope to see it.
Zwarts knew the day and (resolving to put a tricke upon the Cardinall
and his Holinesse), put upon the Passion, in fine water colours the 12
Disciples at Supper, but together by the eares, like the Lapithæ and
Centaures, and about flew the potts, dishes, meate and all; only the
Saviour interposing to make peace among them.   At the time appointed
come the Pope and Cardinal to see this rare piece.   Zwarts carries
them where it hunge, they stood amazed, and thought the painter
madde.   At last sayes the Cardinal, " Goodman Foole, call you this a
Passion ? "   " Yes, 'faith," says he, " and a good one too ; I beleeve
you nere saw the like in your life."   " I thinke so too," sayes the Cardinall, " but, Sirrha, show me the peece I sawe when I was last here."
" Why this is it," sayth Zwarts, " and I have no other finish't in the
house."   The Cardinall denyde it; he swore 'twas true—the Pope
laught to see the braule.   " But," sayes Zwarts, " your Holinesse has
seene my Lord Cardinall's passion ; now I'le show you our Saviour's :
only be pleased to absent yourselves a little out of this roome, and before you examine and observe well the table of this picture, and if you
please leave a servant with me."

They did so, and were no sooner out, but Zwarts, having prepared a
spunge and warme water, immediately expunges all the Historie in
water colours, and (under them) calling for the Pope and Cardinall, presents them with a most lively and doleful picture of our Saviour's Passion.   They runne to the table, examine private markes, find them
there, and are assured by their servant it is the same.   They stand
astonished, judge Zwarts a negromancer, and such a change impossible

without the divell; till at last their gentleman unfolds the riddle, and then they admire both Zwarts his witte and worke.

L'Estrange, No. 310. Mr. Stettkin.

Tricks played by painters upon their friends and patrons are very favourite subjects in several of the popular story books of the Germans. In the old Poem of " Phaffe Amis," printed by Benecke in his " Beyträge," ii. 499 *et seq.* we have an instance of this, where the priest assumes the character of a painter ; and another occurs in the world-renowned " Tyll Eulenspiegel, or Owlglass ; " a new edition of the history of whose adventures, it may here be remarked, has lately been printed at Stuttgart, 12mo, 1838, as the first of a series of the German " Volksbucher," and which is illustrated with some very clever engravings from Ramberg's well-known etchings in outline.

NO. LXVIII.—A.-SLEEPE AND A-WAKE.

Anthony Sleepe of Trinitie, and Wake of Keyes College, used to have many encounters at the taverne ; but Wake never had the better at the witt unlesse he had it at the wine, and then he us'd to crye out, " O Tony, melior Vigilantia Somno."

L'Estrange, No. 312. Mr. Narford.

Wood in his " Fasti Oxonienses," i. 345, ed. Bliss, speaking of Anthony Sleep, has recorded a saying of King James, which may be very appropriately introduced here. " This person, who was a member of Trinity College, Cambridge, was so excellent an orator that he gave King James I. occasion several times to say, that Is. Wake, Orator of the University of Oxon, had a good Ciceronian stile ; but his utterance and manner was so grave, that when he spake before him he was apt to *sleep;* but Sleep, the Deputy Orator of Cambridge, was quite contrary, for he never spake but he kept him awake and made him apt to laugh."—The Wake of our present anecdote is a Cambridge man, probably the Mr. Wake, of Gonville and Caius College, who represented the two characters of " Cola, monachus," and " Pyropus, vestiarius," in the first performance of Ignoramus before the King at Cambridge in 1614-15, and was one of the " loving friends " to whom Ruggle, the author of that Comedy, bequeathed a ring.—(Progr. of K. James, iii. 54.)

NO. LXIX.—A GOOD REASON.

Mr. Pricke, minister of Denham, went to visite one of his sicke parishoners, and ask't him how he did? " O very ill, Sir." " Why how hast thou rested ? " " Oh wondrous ill, for mine eyes have not

come together these three nights." " Why, what's the reason of that?"
" Alas, Sir," sayes he, " because my nose was betwixt them."

L'Estrange, No. 315. Dr. Garnons.

NO. LXX.—THE LAW AND THE GOSPEL.

One Dr. Warren, a divine in degree and profession, yet seldome in
the pulpitt or church; but a justice of peace and very pragmaticall in
secular businesse; having a fellow before him good refractorie, and
stubborne, " Well, Sirrha," sayes he, " goe your wayes. I 'le teach
you law, I 'le warrant you." " Sir," sayes he, " I had rather your
worshippe would teach us some Gospell."

L'Estrange, No. 317. Dr. Garnons.

An entry in Evelyn's Diary gives ground for hope that Dr. Warren amended his practice
in this respect. " October 24, 1686," writes Evelyn, " Dr. Warren preached before the
Princesse at Whitehall, on 5 Matthew, of the blessednesse of the pure in heart, most ele-
gantly describing the blisse of the beatifical vision."—(Evelyn's Diary, iv. 217.)

NO. LXXI.—DOCTOR COLLINS.

Doctor Collins, preaching at St. Marie's about <i>blind</i> obedience,
quoted this text: " If thy right eye offend thee, plucke it out," &c.

L'Estrange, No. 320. Mr. Narford.

The Dr. Collins, who is referred to in this place, and also in two former anecdotes (Nos.
xxv. and lxi.), was a man of great learning and no little wit, son of Baldwyn Collins, whom
Queen Elizabeth used to call Father Collins. He was educated at Eton, and elected from
thence to King's College, Cambridge, under circumstances which gave great token of future
eminence. In 1615 he was chosen Provost of his College, and two years afterwards was
raised to the chair of Regius Professor of Divinity, both which preferments he held until the
breaking out of the Rebellion. He was then sequestered and deprived for refusing to take
the covenant; and, after a few years of retirement, died at Cambridge in 1651, leaving " a
name famous ..... in every Protestant University in Christendom." See Walker's Sufferings of the Clergy, part ii. p. 150; Wood's Athenæ, ii. p. 663, Bliss's ed.

NO. LXXII.—A RURAL DEAN.

One, declaring the analogie betwixt lay and divine officers, sayd a Rurall Deane was an Ecclesiasticall High Constable.

L'Estrange, No. 322. Dr. Garnons.

The very analogy here suggested has been contended for by Kennett, in his " Parochial Antiquities," ii. 337, when he represents the rural dean in the church as answering to the tything man in the state. The Rev. William Dansey, in his recently published " Horæ Decanicæ Rurales," i. 99, proves the incorrectness of Kennett's position.

NO. LXXIII.—NOT A MERRY ANDREW.

Andrew Downes was a great Græcian, and a good scholler, but a very ordinarie man in a pulpitt; and preaching once at St. Marye's was pittifully out, insomuch that he observed some to jeere him. Well, he rubb'd thorough, and gave them a short benediction; but, as he came downe from the pulpitt, " By ——," sayes he, " I 'le never come here againe."

L'Estrange, No. 324. Dr. Garnons.

Andrew Downes, of St. John's, Cambridge, the friend of Camden, and one of the most learned men of his day, was, as Anthony Wood expresses it, " a walking library," and Professor of Greek at Cambridge, affording one of the few instances in which that professorship has not been filled up from Trinity College. He was the author of several learned works, and one of the translators of the Bible.

NO. LXXIV.—ADVICE WELL RECEIVED.

Sleepe being offer'd a small living in the countrie (of little better valew then his fellowshippe) if he would leave the Colledge, and advising at the taverne with his friend what to doe, at last he sent for his horse and resolv'd to goe see it. But just as he was passing out of towne, the sheriefe of the countie was comming, and his trumpetters sounded before him. Sleepe turnes his horse and home againe presently to the taverne. His friends wond'red at his quicke returne, and

ask't him the reason ? " Why, in faith," sayes he, " as I was going
out of towne I heard a voice in the ayre crye, ' Tarry-tony—tarry-
tony—tarry-tony; ' and away came I to my good fellowshippe again."

L'Estrange, No. 325. Dr. Garnons.

To see the force of Sleepe's jest, it must be remembered, that his name was Anthony; and
though, Whittington-like, he fancied he heard the voice of his good genius in the sounds
which by chance fell upon his ear, and when the trumpets cried, " Tarry, Tony ! " determined to take their advice, the character given to him by King James, and which is quoted
in the note to No. LXVII, prevents our applying to him the words of the old song,

" As the bell tinks,
So the fool thinks."

NO. LXXV.—PINCHBACKE PUT TO A PINCH.

Old Jack Pinchbacke, a gamster and rufler in London, came into an
ordinarie very brave, and daub'd with gold lace, and, spying a country
gentleman there, resolved to whett his witt upon him for that meale,
and so seated himselfe by him; meate was no sooner upon the table
but the gentleman boards the best dish before him : " Soft, friend,"
sayes Pinchbacke, " in such places as these, give gentlemen of qualitie
and your betters leave to be before you." " Say you so ? " sayes he ;
" why, they tell me in the country, that when a man comes into an
ordinarie at London, everie man is his owne carver, and eates what he
has a mind to." " O no," sayes Pinchbacke, " take it from me, 'tis
false doctrine." The gentleman being both wise and daring, and well
enough acquainted with the fashions of London, dissembled himselfe ;
and observing that Pinchbacke lov'd his palate, as soone as the second
course was set downe, he had the first hand upon a pheasant. " Fye,"
sayes Pinchbacke, " before —— these country clownes neither know
nor will learne good manners." He held his pheasant for all that, and
fedde as fast upon it as Pinchbacke scof't and play'de upon him; still
answering that in the country he nere heard of any such fashions.
Well, dinner was no sooner done, and the company risen, but this

country gentleman, well flesh't with the best meate, comes boldly up to Pinchbacke: " I prythee," sayes he, " whose Foole art thou ? " Sayes Pinchbacke, " What's thy meaning, friend, by that ? " " Why," sayes he, " by the loose libertie of thy tongue, and (shaking on him by the shoulder) by this garded coate, I take the for some great man's Foole ; but, by G—, if thou beest not somebodyes Foole, I must beate thee. Therefore, if thou wantest that protection, meete me in St. George's Fields, an houre hence, and I'le teach you new ethicks, how to eate your owne sword or mine." Pinchbacke saw him so daring and resolute, wounde himselfe off by an handsome acknowledgment, and the interposing of the company, and very glad he got so rid of him.

L'Estranye, No. 327. Sir Jo. Dalton.

" Old Jack Pinchbacke," as he is here styled, is no doubt the Mr. John Pinchbacke men- tioned by Osborne, in a passage which the reader will find quoted in the note to No. cxxvii.

NO. LXXVI.—A JUSTICE BUT NO JUDGE.

Sir Edward Peyton, at an assizes in Cambridgeshire, all the justices dining together, when the table was cleared and meate taken away, " Gentlemen," says he, " there was one thing troubled me in my bedd all this morning, and I tumbled and tost about it, but am not in all points yet satisfyed ; and that is, whether a *Felo de se* may not have his booke ? I have runn through most of the law, both common and civill, of this kingdome, and know the judges' opinions to be generally against it ; yet I have found out some arguments and reasons which perswade me against them all, that a *Felo de se* may be allowde his booke, or clergy." They, to nourish his folly, gave him leave to recite some of his simple arguments, till he grew so absurd as they could not conteine laughing and jeering of him out of the roome.

L'Estrange, No. 328. Sir Giles Allington.

The Peytons are an ancient Cambridgeshire family.   Sir Edward Peyton, the wise justice of this and the following anecdote, was son and heir of Sir John Peyton, created a Baronet on

the 22nd May 1611. He married thrice, and by his second wife was connected with the
county of Norfolk, which probably brought him under the notice of the collector of these
anecdotes. He died in April 1657. (See that useful volume, Courthope's Extinct Baronetage,
p. 155.) The privilege of the book, or benefit of clergy, has been already alluded to in the
note to No. i.

<hr>

NO. LXXVII.—MUCH JUSTICE AND LITTLE LAW.

There was a businesse that could not be acted by a single justice, yet
Sir Edward Peyton, as a prerogative asse, would needs convent the
parties before him; one, being a shrewd understanding plaine fellow,
told him he thought his worshippe was mistaken, for one justice was
not sufficiente for the business : " Why, Sirrha," sayes he, " am not I
a justice of the peace ? "   " Yes, an 't please your worshippe."   " And
am not I a justice of the quorum ? "   " Yes, Sir."   " Why then,
Sirra," sayes he, " there 's two justices for you,"—and so he entered
like a foole into the cause.

L'Estrange, No. 329. Sir Giles Allington.

<hr>

NO. LXXVIII.—A NEW-MADE KNIGHT.

One Fitz-Jeoffries, being brought up a back-stayer to the King to be
knighted, was turned out another way, to passe through the presence
chamber, which he enter'd with his cappe on his head, and many of the
nobilitie and court being there bare, and he, like the Ægyptian asse,
thinking they did " Sir reverence " the new knight, he came to them
very courteously, and desir'd them to be cover'd, for truly 'twas more
than he expected at their hands, though his Majestie had confer'd a
great honour upon him.   They thank't him very kindly, and desir'd to
be excus'd, for they knew their dutyes, and so long as he was in the
roome they would not be cover'd : upon that away goes the foole, so
puft and swolne with his new honour, as when he comes home he

stuffes the cloathes he was knighted in, and hangs them up in his hall
for ensignes and monuments of an incomparable coxcombe; worthy to
be begged by his respective Gentlemen of the Presence Chamber.

L'Estrange, No. 333. Dr. Garnons.

i. e. to be begged for a fool; *vide ante*, No. XII. Everybody recollects Shakspeare's illustration of the effects of " new-made honour." The only knight of this name dubbed by
James the First, was Sir George Fitz-Jeffrey, who arrived at this dignity at Royston, in the
month of March 1606-7.

NO. LXXIX.—A NEW USE FOR AN OLD HABIT.

Hoskins us'd to call Serjeant Hecham his ape, because of his writhen
face and sneering looke; and one day, the lawyers being merry together,
one ask't his brother Hecham when he would marry? " Never," sayes
he, " I had rather leade apes in hell." " Nay, 'faith," sayes Hoskins,
" if it comes to that once, I am sure thou wilt pose all the devils, for
there will be such gaping and enquiring which is the man, which is the
ape; and they can never distinguish, unless thou goest thither in thy
serjeant's robes."   *L'Estrange, No. 336. My Couz. Pament.*

John Hoskins, (himself a Serjeant) alike eminent as a lawyer, a poet, and as the companion
of Camden, Selden, Raleigh, Jonson, and all the eminent men of that illustrious period.
He revised Raleigh's " History " before it was sent to press; and performed similar offices
for Jonson, who used to call him " father Hoskyns," and say of him, " 'twas he that polished
me; I do acknowledge it." " He was a person," says Anthony Wood, " always pleasant
and facete in company, which made him much desired by ingenious men." (Athenæ Oxon.
ii. 624, ed. Bliss.) He was grandfather to Sir John Hoskins, one of the early members and,
for a time, President of the Royal Society.

The other person in this anecdote was Sir Robert Hitcham, a Suffolk man, educated at the
Free School, Ipswich, and some time of Pembroke Hall. He was of Gray's Inn, called to
the degree of Serjeant-at-law in 1614, and in 1616 appointed the King's Senior Serjeant.
He died 15th August 1636, in the 64th year of his age. His " writhen face and sneering
look," which, be it remarked, do not at all appear in his engraved portrait prefixed to Loder's
History of Framlingham, probably covered a kind heart; for he left a large estate, including
the manor and castle of Framlingham in Suffolk, to Pembroke Hall, for various charitable
purposes. " Hitcham's men," as the inhabitants of his almshouses are termed, must be
well known to every one who has ever passed through Framlingham, distinguished as they

are by their long blue coats with the founder's arms upon the left shoulder. Besides the almshouses, Sir Robert's will provided for the erection and maintenance of a school. He lies in Framlingham Church; and his simple and elegant monument, a black marble slab, supported upon the shoulders of four angels, takes its station, not unworthily, by the side of the more elaborate memorials of the Howards, the former possessors of Framlingham Castle. —(Vide Loder's History of Framlingham, 203, 303.)

NO. LXXX.—DRINKING DEEP.

One ask't Sir John Millesent how he did so conforme himselfe to the grave justices his brothers, when they mett. "Why, in faith," sayes he, "I have no way but to drinke myselfe downe to the capacitie of the Bench." *L'Estrange, No.* 337. *My Couz. Pament.*

In that scandalous chronicle of the times, Weldon's Court of James, Sir Anthony, after exhibiting a curious picture of the ridiculous follies in which the King found amusement, adds, "But Sir John Millicent, who was never known before, was commended for notable fooling; and was indeed the best extemporary fool of them all." Sir John Millesent was knighted at Royston, Jan. 20, 1606-7; his estates were at Barham in Cambridgeshire. (See **Lysons's** Magna Britannia, Cambr. p. 320.)

NO. LXXXI.—INACCURACY OF EARLY LONDON EDITIONS
OF THE BIBLE.

Dr. Usher, Bishop of Armath, being to preach at Paule's Crosse, and passing hastily by one of the Stationers, call'd for a Bible, and had a little one of the London edition given him out; but when he came to looke for his text, that very verse was omitted in the print; which gave the first occasion of complaints to the King of the insufferable negligence and insufficiencie of the London printers and presse, and bredde that great contest that followed betwixt the University of Cambridge and London Stationers about printing of the Bibles.

L'Estrange, No. 348. *Dr. Garnons.*

A good deal of interesting matter, illustrative of this anecdote, will be found in D'Israeli's " Curiosities of Literature." The story before us did not escape the researches of that amusing writer.

NO. LXXXII.—THE BITERS BIT.

Sir Thomas Jermin, meaning to make himselfe merry, and gull the Cockers, sends his man into the Pitt in Shoo Lane, with an £100 and a dunghill cocke, neatly trimmed and cutt for the battell. The plot being well layd, the fellow gets another to throw him in and fight him in Sir Thomas Jermin's name, and the fellow beates the £100 against him. The cocke was match't, and bearing Sir Thomas Jermin's name, had many beates on his head; but after three or four good brushes, he shewe a faire payre of heeles. Every one wond'red to see Sir Thomas his streine cry Craven; and away came his man with his mony doubled.

L'Estrange, No. 352. *Sir Jo. Pooly.*

Sir Thomas Jermin has been already noticed under No. LIII. We here see that, even in the so called "good old times," sporting noblemen did not disdain to make money by "practices not worshipful."

NO. LXXXIII.—AN UNSAVOURY SUIT.

Sir Roger Williams (who was a Welchman, and but a taylour at first, though afterwards a very brave souldier,) being gracious with Queen Elizabeth, prefer'd a sute to her, which she thought not fitt to grant; but he, impatient of a repulse, resolv'd to give another assault; so coming one day to court, makes his addresse to the Queene, and watching his time, when she was free and pleasant, beganne to move againe; she perceived it at the instant, and observing a new payre of boots on his leggs, clapps her hand to her nose and cryes, "Fah, Williams, I pr'y-the begone, thy bootes stinke." "Tut, tut, Madame," sayes he, "'tis my sute that stinkes." *L'Estrange, No.* 357. *Mr. Potts.*

The following account of this valiant Welshman appears in Camden's "History of Queen Elizabeth," p. 507, ed. 1675: "In the same month (Dec. 1595), departed this life Sir Roger Williams, Knight, a Welshman, of the family of Penrose in Monmouthshire, who first was a souldier of fortune, under the Duke of Alva; and afterward, having happily run through all the parts of military discipline, might have been compared with the most famous captains of the age, could he have tempered the heat of his warlike spirit with more wariness and prudent discretion. In this certainly he excelled many, that being a rude and unlearned man, and only taught by experience, he wrote with exquisite judgment the History of the Low Country Wars, at which he was present; and in an excellent book hath maintained the military art now practised, and in use before that of former ages, not at all pleasing thereby the old souldiers and lovers of archery. At his funeral in St. Paul's Church, the Earl of Essex was present in mourning, and as many military officers as were then in the city." The books mentioned by Camden, as written by Sir Roger Williams, are : " A Brief Discourse of Warre, written by Sir Roger Williams, Knight, with his opinion concerning some parts of the Martial Discipline," London, 1590, 4to. ; and, " The Actions of the Low Countries," London, 1618, 4to.

NO. LXXXIV.—THE CASE IS CHANGED.

Francis Quarles had bespoken a lute case, and upon leaving the Inns of Court, and going into the country, call'd for it, and ask't what he must pay? 20s. sayes the workman. " Faith," sayes he, " I have not so much mony about me, and I am now going away; but if thou wilt take my case for thy case (meaning his Inn-of-Court gowne that he had-then on), 'tis a match." And so they agreed upon the bargaine.

L'Estrange, No. 360. *Tho. Brew.*

Francis Quarles, the poet, and author of the well-known " Emblems," was of an ancient family, and nephew to Sir Robert Quarles. He was educated at Christ's College, Cambridge, and studied at Lincoln's Inn. He afterwards became successively Cup-bearer to the Queen of Bohemia, Secretary to the Primate of Ireland, and Chronologer to the City of London.

NO. LXXXV.—A MUSICAL DISCORD.

Jack Willson and Harry and Will: Lawes were at a taverne one night. Wilson being in worst case of the three, swore he would quarrell with the next man he mett, who was a meere stranger, and a sober gentleman; whome he thus accosted, " Are not you a Catholicke?" " Yes, marry am I." " Then y' are a knave," sayes he. The gentleman having pass't by a little way, stepps backe to him and bids him not swallow an error; " for," sayes he, " I am no Catholicke." " Why, then, y' are a scurvy lying knave," sayes Willson. Upon that out flew their swords, but the Lawes parted them presently.

L'Estrange, No. 361. *Tho. Brew.*

Dr. John Wilson, who appears, like Falstaff, to have been styled " Jack " by his familiars, was not only an able composer, but in his time esteemed the best performer on the lute in England. He was created Musical Doctor at Oxford in 1644, and was preferred to the chair of Musical Professor in 1656. He was a man of a facetious temper ; and styled by Anthony Wood, " a great humourist, and a pretender to buffoonery." Henry Lawes, his companion in the present drunken frolic, has given, says Hawkins (iv. 59), a much more amiable, and probably a truer, portrait of him in the following lines, part of a Poem prefixed to Wilson's " Psalterium Carolinum, the Devotion of His Sacred Majesty in his Solitudes and Sufferings, rendred in verse. Set to music for three voices and an organ, or theorbo. Fol. 1657."

> " From long acquaintance and experience, I
> Could tell the world thy known integrity
> Unto thy friend ; thy true and honest heart,
> Ev'n mind, good nature, all but thy great art,
> Which I but dully understand —

This is good evidence from —

> " Harry, whose tuneful and well-measured song "

won him the friendship of Milton.

Wilson was the composer of a glee for three voices, published in " Playford's Musical Companion," where the words are attributed to Shakspeare ; and the supposition that they were really written by him, having been converted into a certainty, by their appearing with Shakspeare's name to them in the MS. Collection of Poetry, copied prior to 1631 by Richard Jackson, mentioned by Mr. Collier, in his " Annals of the Stage," iii. 275, they are here reprinted (never having been inserted in any collection of Shakspeare's Poems), and may, without any great exercise of poetical licence, be styled—

A SONG FOR AUTOLYCUS.

> From the fair Lavinian shore,
> I your markets come to store ;
> Muse not, though so far I dwell,
> And my wares come here to sell.
> Such is the *sacred hunger for gold !*
> Then come to my pack,
> While I cry,
> What d' ye lack ?
> What d' ye buy ?
> For here it is to be sold.
>
> I have beauty, honour, grace,
> Fortune, favour, time, and place,

H

50   ANECDOTES AND TRADITIONS.

And what else thou would'st request,
E'en the thing thou likest best ;
First let me have but a touch of your gold.
  Then, come to me, lad,
    Thou shalt have
  What thy dad
    Never gave,
For here it is to be sold.

Madam, come see what you lack,
I've complexions in my pack ;
White and red you may have in this place,
To hide your old and wrinkled face.
First let me have but a touch of your gold,
    Then you shall seem
    Like a girl of fifteen,
Although you be threescore and ten years old.

My late respected friend Mr. Douce once told me, that some musical friend at Chichester.
I think the organist, possessed a copy of this song with an additional verse.

NO. LXXXVI.—A PUN OF POLICY.

When the feares were of warres with Scotland, and every one inquisitive, as Marquis Hamilton returned from thence, and past English townes, every one ask't his followers : " What newes? " but their answere was allwayes " Peace, peace ; " which left all doubtfull still, the word importing both accord and silence, for men were inhibited discourse and enquirie of Scottish affaires.   *L'Estrange, No.* 368. *Mr. Harris.*

This anecdote evidently refers to the circumstances of the years 1638 and 1639, during which the Marquess of Hamilton passed to and fro between the Court of England and Edinburgh, the head quarters, if not the court of the Covenanters. (Vide Burnet's Memoirs of the Dukes of Hamilton, pp. 65 and 111, edit. 1677.) For some time after the union of the two Crowns, the affairs of Scotland lost all their ancient interest in the eyes of Englishmen. Clarendon, in a striking passage, pourtrays the total disregard into which they had fallen ; " The truth is there was so little curiosity, either in the court or the country, to know any thing of Scotland or what was done there, that when the whole nation was sollicitous to know what passed weekly in Germany and Poland, and all other parts of Europe, no man ever enquir'd what was going on in Scotland, nor had that kingdom a place or mention in one page of any Gazette." (Clar. Rebell. i. 110.)—The inhabitants of England were aroused from this slumber by learning, not only that the Scottish nation had been driven into rebellion by their dislike to what they termed the rags and remnants of popery, but that they were preparing to maintain their own freedom by pouring an army into Northumberland. " And this," says Clarendon, " was the first alarm England receiv'd towards any trouble, after it had enjoy'd for so many years the most uninterrupted prosperity, in a full and plentiful peace, that any nation could be bless'd with." (Ibid. 113.)

NO. LXXXVII.—VERY HUNGRY INDEED.

Sayes one that was very empty and hungry, " If I gett not some victuals, my stomach gnawes so, as I thinke it will eate me up."
L'Estrange, No. 370. My Sis. Ka. Lewk.

Hungry as this gentleman appears to have been, his appetite might probably have been stayed, had he eaten the oyster lately described in one of the American papers, as being so large that it *took three men to swallow it whole.*

NO. LXXXVIII.—CATHEDRAL MUSIC.

One comming into a cathedrall, whose quire consisted of very ill voices, and made a lamentable noise, said, " Sure the prophecy of Amos was there fulfilled, cap. viii. v. 3 : And the songs of the temple shall be howlings."   *L'Estrange, No. 373. Anonymus.*

NO. LXXXIX.—A MERRY TRANSLATOR.

One sayd merrily, that " Inter Calicem supremaque labra," was in English betwixt Dover and Calice—the promontorie of Dover being " Angliæ Suprema Labra."
L'Estrange, No. 374. Anonymus.

No doubt the same gentleman who translated that passage in Cæsar which describes him as proceeding into Gaul, " summâ diligenciâ "—*on the top of the diligence!*

NO. XC.—COKE VERSUS GUNPOWDER.

Upon the Powder Plott, when Faux came to his examination, and was pinch't very close with an interrogatorie of Sir Edward Cook's, and demur'd long, yet falter'd much in his answere. " Nay," sayes Sir Edward Cooke, " this is *Mille Testes* when it comes once to a *Vox Faucibus*, or *Faux vocibus hæret*."

L'Estrange, No. 375. *Anon.*

The Gunpowder Plot gave full scope for the exercise of Coke's professional talent, and not a few opportunities for the display of his singular style of wit. The following passage in his speech upon the trial of Fawkes is not only as excellent a specimen as could be produced of the merits and defects of Coke's eloquence, but contains also another application of the quotation upon which his joke in the above anecdote turns. " Miserable desolation ! no King, no Queen, no Issue Male, no Councillors of State, no Nobility, no Bishops, no Judges ! O, barbarous, and more than Scythian or Thracian cruelty ! No mantle of holiness can cover it ! no pretence of religion can excuse it ; no shadow of good intention can extenuate it ; God and heaven condemn it — man and earth detest it — the offenders themselves were ashamed of it—wicked people exclaim against it—and the souls of all true Christian subjects abhor it. Miserable, but yet sudden had their ends been, who should have died in that fiery tempest and storm of gunpowder ; but more miserable had they been that had escaped : and what horrible effects the blowing up of so much powder and stuff would have wrought not only amongst men and beasts, but even upon insensible creatures, churches, and houses, and all places near adjoining, you who have been martial men best know—for myself, *Vox faucibus hæret*." (State Trials, ii. 177.) It was in the same speech that he gave his well-known version of S. P. Q. R. *Stultus Populus quærit Romam* (Ibid. 181), and said of the Jesuits, that they did not " watch and pray," but " watched *to prey*." (Ibid. 182.)

NO. XCI.—A LATIN TOAST.

Mr. Harrison, Vice Master of Trinitie Colledge, a very reverend, grave, and facetious cheerful man, who delighted both to speake and to be answered in elegant Latine, allwayes gave his tost to be tosted with this phrase : " Admoveatur igni donec in utrumque latus erubescat."

L'Estrange, No. 377. *Mr. Greene.*

NO. XCII.—DOUBLE DAMAGES.

A fellow was censured to the pillorie, and his head being in, he raised himselfe on his tippe-toes, and the foot-ledge brake, being old, rotten, and disus'd, and there the poore wretch hung by the necke in danger of his life; after his penance, he brings his action against the towne for the insufficiencie of their pillorie, and recovers against them.

L'Estrange, No. 387. *Dr. Lewin.*

Representations of various forms of the ancient pillory may be seen in Douce's Illustrations of Shakspeare, i. 146; and Strutt's Horda, i. pl. 15; ii. pl. 1.

NO. XCIII.—NO UPRIGHT JUDGE.

Judge Richardson, in going the Westerne Circuite, had a great flint stone throwne at his head by a malefactor, then condemned, (who thought it meritorious, and the way to be a benefactor to the Common-wealth, to take away the life of a man so odious,) but leaning low of his elbow, in a lazie recklesse manner, the bullett flew too high and only tooke off his hatt. Soone after, some friends congratulating his deli-verance, he replyde, by way of jeast (as his fashion was to make a jeast of every thing), " You see now, if I had beene an upright Judge (intimating his reclining posture) I had been slaine."

L'Estrange, No. 394. *My Bro. Spring.*

Sir Thomas Richardson, Chief Justice of the Common Pleas, and afterwards of the King's Bench, and Speaker of the House of Commons in the last Parliament of James I. He was born at Mulbarton in Norfolk, a county which Fuller has described as having a great reputation for litigiousness. Beyond doubt it has produced many able lawyers, which may have given rise to the opinion, that men there study law at the plough-tail. (Fuller's Worthies, ii. 126.) Richardson, after passing through the rank of King's Serjeant, was appointed to the Chief Justiceship of the Common Pleas on the 28th November 1626, and removed to the King's Bench 24th October 1631. He died in 1634, and was buried in Westminster Abbey. He is described by Lloyd (State Worthies, 976), as " humoursom but honest." Of his jokes recorded in other places besides the present MS. the most noted is one made upon leaving the Council, where he had been reprimanded by Laud for an endeavour to suppress Sunday wakes and revels. Neal says, the reprimand "almost broke his heart" (Hist. of Puritans, ii. 213) ; however that might be, it certainly did not deprive him of his power of breaking jokes, for as he passed out he declared that the lawn sleeves had almost choked him.

NO. XCIV.—A CUP TOO MUCH.

Bishoppe Wrenne, a mightie man in ceremonies, and in deadly opposition to the towne of Ipswich, hearing that Mountague, Bishop of Norwich, (a man good-indifferent, and indulgent in those points,) passing that way was graciously (courteously) entertained, and presented with a Gilt Cuppe ; wrote him a scorning letter upon it, insinuating that he heard he tooke a Cuppe too much at Ipswich, and was sorry for him he should be so much overseene.

L'Estrange, No. 395. My Bro. Spring.

The dislike between Matthew Wren, Bishop of Norwich, and afterwards of Ely, and the town of Ipswich seems to have been mutual, and the town had the better of the quarrel, at any event for many years, for upon their petition the Commons impeached the Bishop, and he was confined in the Tower for eighteen years. Cromwell offered to release him, but in that case he must have acknowledged the Protector's authority, which was a condition to which the old man would not submit. Shortly before the Restoration, he was discharged from imprisonment, and died at Ely House, April 24, 1667, in the 82nd year of his age. He was uncle to Sir Christopher Wren.

NO. XCV.—NINEPENCES AND HARPERS.

There was a good merry fellow, and musicall, but naturally somewhat doubled about the backe ; and his comrades usually call'd him their Ninepence and their Harper : because commonly ninepences are a little buckled to distinguish in their currancie up and downe, least they passe (some being bigge, some small) for a sixpence or a shilling.

L'Estrange, No. 396. Anonymous.

The shillings of Ireland, which bore the figure of a harp, as the emblem of that country, were familiarly called Harpers, and their value was only ninepence, " a fourth part less than sterling English."—(Ruding's Annals of the Coinage, 4to, 1817, ii. 253.)

NO. XCVI.—A QUESTION OF PRECEDENCY.

Mountague Bishop of Norwich, inveighing at his owne table against the courses of Henry the Eighth, swore that if there were a triumvirate in hell, Judas had the first, Julian the second, and Henry the VIII. the third place; and, had he not fallen short in time, undoubtedly had had the primacie.   *L'Estrange, No.* 398. *My Father.*

Dr. Richard Montague, whose publications entitled, "*A new Gag for an old Goose,*" and "*An Appeal to Cæsar,*" were subjects of inquiry in the first parliament of Charles I. His prosecution by the Commons was a passport to favour at Court, and he was successively appointed to the Bishoprics of Chichester and Norwich. His death on April 12, 1641, saved him from the resentment of the long Parliament.

NO. XCVII.—GOOD ADVICE.

A grave gentleman in this kingdome us'd this phrase often : " Do nothing rashly, but catching of fleas."

L'Estrange, No. 405. *Mr. Calthorpe.*

NO. XCVIII.—DECLINING THE ARTICLES.

When the New Oath Canons and Articles were so violently urg'd by the clergie, and so much slighted and spurn'd at by most, the Bishop of London visiting and coming into a church, with the Mace carryed before him, ask't one of the churchwardens if he would sweare to the Articles. The man, being a plaine blunt fellow, " No, Sir," says he, " not I, an grace of God, for all your Artichoke there,"—meaning the coronet of the mace, resembling one.

L'Estrange, No. 406. *My Father.*

The canons referred to are those of the Synod of 1640, containing " the new oath," which was ridiculed as the *et cetera* oath, from its comprising a declaration of consent to the government of the church, by Archbishops, Bishops, Deans, and Archdeacons, &c. The Bishop alluded to was the mild and pious Juxon.

NO. XCIX.—A BOX OF WHISTLES.

When the Scotts invaded the Northerne parts, 1640, a Sergeant Major was billetted in one Mr. Calvert's house, who was musically dispos'd, and had a portative organ for his pleasure in one of his chambers. The Scotch man being of the preciser straine, and seeing the instrument open, " Art tou a Kirkman?" sayes he. " No, Sir," sayes he. " Den what a Dele, mon, dos't tou with this same great Boax of Whistles here?" *L'Estrange, No. 407. My Father.*

Portativi, or regals, were a kind of diminutive portable organ, formerly much used in public processions. Hawkins speaks of this instrument as being not uncommon in Germany even in his day. The regal was borne through the streets on a man's shoulders ; when the procession stopped, it was set down upon a stool ; the performer then stepped forward, played upon it, and the man that carried it blew the bellows.—(Hawkins, ii. 449.)

I am indebted for this quotation to Mr. Dauney's admirable volume, " The Ancient Melodies of Scotland," one of the most interesting works on the subject of musical history which has appeared of late years ; and in which, p. 116, may be found the following illustration of the new name bestowed in this anecdote upon the organ, " The whistle is the popular appellation in Scotland for every species of flute, fife, or flageolet."

NO. C.—ELIZABETHAN FREEMASONRY.

Charles Chester, a Court Foole in Queen Elizabeth's time, us'd to be girding very often at my Lord Knolls and Sir Walter Raleigh. Sayes Sir Walter Raleigh, " My Lord, gett but this foole to dinner one day, and you shall see what a tricke wee 'le serve him." So he did ; and when his paunch was well fill'd (for he was a notable trencher-man), and he went out of the chamber, Sir Walter Raleigh followed him. " Come, Sirrah," sayes he, " now wee'l be revenged on you for all your rogerie ;" and having some servants by, tyed him hand and foote, sett him right up in a corner, called a mason or two, built him up presently to the chinne, and so close as he could not move, and threat'ned to cover him in, but that he begg'd hard and swore he would abuse them no more ; so they lett him stand till night.

L'Estrange, No. 412. Phill. Calth.

We have here a name, which has hitherto, we believe, remained unrecorded, added to those of Pace, Clod, and the other jesters who flourished in the time, and at the Court of Elizabeth; for though it will be seen from the following extract from Aubrey's Lives, ii. p. 514, where Chester appears likewise as the subject of a practical joke on the part of Sir Walter Raleigh (who is no doubt Aubrey's " Sir W. R.") that he was the original of Ben Jonson's " Carlo Buffone," he has never been known as a court jester. " In his (Jonson's) youthful time was one Charles Chester, that after kept company with his acquaintance; he was a bold impertinent fellowe, and they could never be at quiet for him; a perpetual talker, and made a noyse like a drum in a roome: so one time at a taverne, Sir W. R. beates him and seales up his mouth, i. e. his upper and neather beard, with hard wax. From him Ben Jonson takes his *Carlo Buffone*, in 'Every Man out of his Humour.' "

A tolerably complete list of these motley retainers of the English Court might be compiled; for the succession was scarcely interrupted from the time of Berdic, Joculator Regis, who is mentioned in Domesday, down to that of Tom Killegrew, who Pepys tells us, on the 13th February 1667-8, " hath a fee out of the wardrobe for Cap and Bells, under the title of 'King's Fool or Jester;' and may revile or jeer any body, the greatest person, without offence, by the privilege of his place."

In the lately published and highly interesting volume of M. Rigollot, entitled, " *Monnaies des Fous*," &c. Paris, 1837, we are furnished with another curious fact on this subject, entirely unknown, we believe, to English antiquaries; we mean, the existence at the court of John, of a jester, named Will Picol, or Piculfus, exercising his functions, not *virtute officii*, but " *à titre feodal*," holding his good lands by the tenure of saying good things; the said good lands passing to his heirs, on the payment annually of a pair of golden spurs. The following is a copy of the grant which M. Rigollot has printed by way of satisfying the doubts of the sceptical: —

" *Joannes* .... *D. G. &c. Sciatis nos dedisse et presenti charta confirmasse* Will. Picol, Follo *nostro Fontem Ossane (perhaps* Menil-Ozenne, pays de Mortain) *cum omnibus pertinenciis suis, habend. et tenend. sibi et heredïbus suis, faciendo inde nobis annuatim servicium unius* Folli *quoad vixerit: et post ejus decessum heredes sui eam de nobis tenebunt, et per servicium unius paris calcarium deauratorum nobis annuatim reddendo. Quare volumus et firmiter precipimus quod predict.* Piculfus *et heredes sui habeant et teneant in perpetuum, bene et in pace, libere et quiete, predictam terram, &c.* [Char. circa 1200, Bibl. Reg.]

NO. CI.—A GREAT DIFFERENCE.

In Lynne their Maior is allwayes chosen out of the twelve Aldermen, and they out of eighteen others. One of the eighteen being at Rising (an ancient but decayed burrow-towne), and the then Maior a mechanicke man, a butcher or the like, sayes he: " Mr. Maior, I heare you have a very odd forme and manner of election here of your Maior."

" Why, how is that?" sayes the Maior. " Why, they say for certaine that you and all your brethren goe into a barne, where every man hath his bottle of hey layde him for a cushion : then ther's a calf turn'd in at the barne dore, and looke to what bottle the calfe goe first, hee's the man." " Why then," sayes he, " I see the difference betwixt us and our brethren at Lynne ; wee choose with one calfe, and you with eighteene."   *L'Estrange, No. 423. Bro. Ham.*

An article on various ancient forms of municipal election, particularly at Cambridge, may be seen in the Gentleman's Magazine for April 1839, p. 383.

NO. CII.—NO FEAR OF CHANGE.

When the Lord of Carnarvan was going to travaile, and one bad him take heede he did not change his religion. " Ther's no feare of that," sayes he, " for by ——, no man living will be so madde as to change religions with me."   *L'Estrange, No. 425. Sir W. Spring.*

Whatever might have been at one time the religion of this nobleman, Robert second Baron Dormer, who was created Viscount Ascot and Earl of Carnarvon 1628, his sentiments upon this subject would appear to have undergone a very important change. Granger tells us, on the authority of Fuller, that when he was expiring, after having been run through the body by the hand of a straggling trooper near Newbury, and some nobleman inquired of him whether he had any request to make to the King, Charles I., he replied, " I will not die with a suit in my mouth, but to the King of Kings."

NO. CIII.—HOW TO TAME A KING'S HORSE.

King James mounted his horse one time, who formerly used to be very sober and quiet, but then began to bound and prance. " The de'le o' my saul, Sirrha," sayes he, " an you be not quiet I'se send you to the five hundred kings in the lower House of Commons ; they'le quickly tame you."   *L'Estrange, No. 437. Sir W. Spring.*

NO. CIV.—THE KING OF SPAIN'S HEAD IN DANGER.

One sayde of Sir Francis Drake's expedition into the Indies, that he endangered the King of Spaine's head shrewdly, when he singed his beard so there. *L'Estrange, No. 446. My Father.*

Many very interesting particulars of Drake, and of his expeditions, to which he was as much incited by the desire " to lick himself whole of the damage he had received of the Spaniards," as by a feeling of patriotism, are contained in Camden's " History of Queen Elizabeth."

NO. CV.—RELIGIOUS EQUALITY.

Parson Edmund Gourny, inveighing against the common fault of the meaner sort of people, who are too prone to performe civill and outward respects, upon the coming of greater persons into the church, by rising, bowing, &c. sayes he: " I like an holy-rowly-Powlinesse ; for there sure, if any where, we ought to be haile fellows well met."

L'Estrange, No. 451. Edw. Gourny.

Some particulars of this facetious divine have been given in the note to No. xi.

NO. CVI.—AN AWKWARD ARGUMENT.

In very licentious times a notorious offender refus'd to obey a warrant, but was at last brought in by force to Sir Robert Chichly, the justice that sent for him. But the delinquent lay still upon his old guard (which he had bragg'd so much of before) that there was no law now, and he car'd not a fig what any justice could do to him. " Very well, Sirrha," sayes he, " if there be no law then (commanding two or three stout servants about him) fetch me a roape ; " which they did, and nous'd him, and good fiercely began to trusse up, but he presently cryde *peccavi,* and became very obedient to all orders.

L'Estrange, No. 482. Dr. Garnons.

NO. CVII.—THE PRACTICE OF PIETY PREJUDICIAL.

The towne of Tiverton is mentioned as a fearful example of God's judgment for the prophanation of the Sabbath (being twice burnt), in a booke intituled "The Practice of Pietie;" and being a third time burn't, and a brief procured, and a Devonshire man collector, the very memorie of the probable occasion of the former flames cooleth the charitie of many that remembered the storie, and was objected to the collector, who replyed that "there was no truth in it, and the ʿ Practice of Pietie ʾ had done them much wrong"—which words bearing a double sense occasion'd much laughter.   *L'Estrange, No. 453. N. L. S.*

The " Practice of Pietie," the book above referred to, was written by Lewis Bayly, Bishop of Bangor, and first published in 1619, under the title of " The Practice of Piety, being the substance of several Sermons preached at Evesham." It afterwards passed through a long series of editions, that of 1735 being the fifty-ninth ; and it was translated into most of the languages of Protestant Europe. The examples given of " God's judgments by fire " are Stratford-upon-Avon, " twice upon the same day twelve month (being the Lord's day) almost consumed," and Tiverton, as follows :

" Teverton, in Devonshire (whose remembrance makes my heart bleed), was oftentimes admonished by her godly preacher, that God would bring some heavie judgement on the towne for their horrible prophanation of the Lord's day, occasioned chiefly by their market on the day following. Not long after his death, on the third of Aprill anno Dom. 1598, God in lesse than halfe an houre consumed with a sudden and fearefull fire the whole towne, except onely the church, the court-house, and the almes-houses, or a few poore peoples dwellings ; where a man might have seene foure hundred dwelling houses all at once on fire; and above fiftie persons consumed with the flame. And nowe againe, since the former edition of this booke, on the fifth of August last, 1612 (fourteene yeares since the former fire) the whole towne was againe fired and consumed, except some thirtie houses of poore people, with the schoole-house and almes-houses. They are blind which see not in this the finger of God : God grant them grace, when it is next built, to change their market day, and to remove all occasions of prophaning the Lord's day. Let other townes remember the Tower of Siloe, Luke, xiii. 4 ; and take warning by their neighbours' chastisements : Feare God's threatenings, Jeremie xvii. 27 ; and beleeve God's prophets, if they will prosper, 1 Chron. xx. 20."

NO. CVIII.—A REASONABLE MOTION.

A motion being made in the House of Commons that such as were chosen to serve in the Parliament troopes should be faithfull and skillfull riders, Mr. Waller's opinion was demanded, who approved the forme of it as excellent, " for," sayes he, " it is most necessary the riders be faithfull least they runne away with their horses, and skilfull least their horses runne away with them."

L'Estrange, No. 454. Dr. Garnons.

Edmund Waller the poet first sat in parliament for the borough of Agmondesham in 1640. In 1642 he was one of the Commissioners appointed by the Parliament to present their propositions of peace to the King at Oxford; and in the following year was deeply engaged in a design to reduce the City of London and the Tower to the service of the King. After he had saved himself from the consequences of this plot, a full account of which is given both by Whitlocke and Clarendon, he went to France, where he remained some time. On his return he attached himself to Cromwell, which did not prevent him from being very kindly treated by Charles the Second, after whose restoration he sat again in Parliament several times.

NO. CIX.—A PRAYER AMENDED.

At the close of something read by a ballett-monger in the streete, he cryed, " God save the King and the Parliament;" sayes a merry fellow that went by, " God save the King, the Parliament will looke well enough to save themselves." *L'Estrange, No. 455. Anon.*

NO. CX.—COKE'S REPORTS.

Mr. John Coke, sonne to Sir Edward Coke the lawyer, tooke much offence at one that ignorantly wrote him Cooke, not Coke : " Faith," sayes one that stood by, "Any man that ever saw him (for he was a great fellow in large folio) would sweare he should rather be written oo than o." Another sayd of him, in regard of his loud vociferation and bawling at all conferences and meetings, " What an eminent man will this grow if he be long lived, whose *reports* allready so far exceed his father's." *L'Estrange, No. 552. Anon.*

The subject of the present anecdote was the fourth son of the celebrated Lord Chief Justice. He was seated at Holkham, and married Meriel, daughter of Anthony Wheatley, esq. by whom he had six sons and nine daughters. The estate, however, descended to his youngest son John, and he dying unmarried the property devolved upon Henry, the Judge's fifth son.

That the name of his illustrious father was commonly, if not "ignorantly, wrote" *Cooke*, there is abundant evidence. The anecdote No. xxx, which we have already printed, rests entirely upon the fact of his being so called; and Lloyd, in his "State Worthies," designates him the Lord Chief Justice *Cook*—which, in the edition of 1766, is corrected by the Editor in a note to *Coke*. (See Whitworth's edition of Lloyd, ii. 109.)

Even in our day the representative of this family was popularly termed "Cook of Norfolk," until her Majesty honoured him with the well deserved title of Earl of Leicester.

NO. CXI.—THE RETORT UNCOURTEOUS.

A gentleman that had mighty large and retorted Austrian lipps, comming from the barber's, ask't his familiar friend how he lik't his trimming, "Y'faith very well," sayes he, "but that he has turn'd up thy lipps instead of thy beard."   *L'Estrange, No.* 458. *Anon.*

Aubrey, in his "Correspondence," ii. pt. 2, p. 500, who tells us, "Sir Walter Raleigh was a tall, handsome, bold man; but his *næve* was, that he was damnably proud," and that, "he had a most remarkable aspect, an exceeding high forehead, long faced, and sour eyelided," adds, "his beard turned up naturally," a circumstance which gave him no small advantage over the gallants of the time, who, as we learn from this anecdote, were indebted to the barbers for giving their mustachios the fashionable turn.

NO. CXII.—A FAULT NOT TO BE AMENDED.

Young Robert Bacon, being at his uncle's house at Redgrave, and having walk't out one morning with some other gentlemen, they came in upon the front of the house, which was very gracefull, and one of them protested, that of all that ever he saw he never saw a better coming to an house in his life. Robert Bacon swore it was one of the worst in England. "Oh, fye," sayes the other, "what fault can you find in it?" "By ——," sayes he, "it is too longe by halfe," meaning before *his* coming to it.   *L'Estrange, No.* 465. *Sir Jo. Holland.*

"Queen Elizabeth," says Puttenham, "came in one of her Progresses to visit Sir Nicholas Bacon at his house at Redgrave; and said, 'My Lord, how small a house you have.' He replied, 'Madam, my house is not small, but you have made me too great for it.'" It does not, however, appear from the " Progresses of Queen Elizabeth," that her Majesty was ever at Redgrave ; and in vol. ii. of that work, p. 56, Mr. Nichols states that this anecdote belongs to Sir Nicholas Bacon's other mansion at Gorhambury, near St. Alban's ; to which he added wings, it is said, for the specific purpose of accommodating more conveniently the royal train. The expenses of Elizabeth's visit there in 1577, when she stayed for five days, are printed in detail in the same work ; they amount to £577. 6s. 7¼d.

The " young Robert Bacon" of this anecdote was the eldest son of Sir Robert the third Baronet ; and his uncle, in whose lifetime it is dated, was Sir Edmund the second Baronet, the son and heir of " old Sir Nicholas," noticed under No. xlix. The present collection, in addition to No. cxxxi, printed hereafter, contains likewise the following story bearing upon the unthrifty character of " young Robert :"—

" One told Sir Edmund Bacon, he did his nephew Robert (heire to his honour and land, and much in debt), a great deal of wrong in holding out so, and keeping that estate from him which he had so much neede on. ' Alas,' sayes he, ' that 's a fault in nature, for let him never trust to that, for we Bacons alwayes dye upward."—(No. 464, Sir Will. Spring.)

It is no source of regret to find, that the " fault in nature " was not amended in favour of this greedy heir-expectant ; he survived indeed his uncle (who died in 1649) but not his father ; dying on the 25th Aug. 1652, leaving an only son, Edmund, who became the fourth Baronet on his grandfather's death in 1655.

NO. CXIII.—A JUDGE JUDGED.

A most corrupt judge was executed; and an atturney, relating the passages to another, " Alas, poore man," sayes he, " what a solitarie, inglorious, and unsociable end had he." " Why how would you have him dye ? " sayes the Atturney. " I'faith," sayes he, " I would have no man of his condition and profession hang'd but in due equipage ; labelled with an hundred atturneys at least—*Solamen miseris socios habuisse doloris.*"
                                                     L'Estrange, No. 474. *Anon.*

NO. CXIV.—PLAIN BUT WHOLESOME.

Parson Leedes, of Lynne, a good honest plaine preacher, beganne one Sunday with this prologue out of the pulpitt to his auditorie (and the rather because some of them had itching eares). " My brethren, I have no fine manchett for you, but I'le breake a browne loafe amongst you, you shall have *Panem Domini,* and that 's good wholesome foode I can tell you."   *L'Estrange, No.* 481. *Mr. Loades.*

NO. CXV.—EUPHUISM.

A gentleman complimenting with a lady in pure Sir Philip Sidney, she was so well verst in his author, as tacitely she traced him to the bottome of a leafe, where (his memorie failing) he brake off abruptly. " Nay, I beseech you, Sir," sayd she, " proceede and turn over the leafe, for methinke the best part is still behinde;" which unexpected discovery silenc't him for ever after.

L'Estrange, No. 484. Mr. An. Cooke.

The reader will at once perceive, that what is here described as " pure Sir Philip Sidney," is the same as the " Euphuism " spoken of, and admirably illustrated by Sir Walter Scott, in his " Monastery," i. 197, ed. 1830, and " Introduction," and which is so called from " that singularly comcombical work, Euphues and his England, "written by John Lylley, who, if his editor Blount is to be believed, was " the only rare poet of his time, the witty, comical, facetiously-quick, and quickly-facetious ; he that sate at Apollo's table, and to whom Phœbus gave a wreath of his own bays without snatching." They are spoken of as identical by Decker in his Gull's Hornbook, chap. vi. " When the Arcadian and Euphuis'd gentlewomen have their tongues sharpened to set upon you ; " while Drayton seems to speak (Of Poets and Poesy, p. 1256), as if Sir Philip Sydney had put an end to Euphuism, though a perusal of the Arcadia convinces us he was by no means justified in doing so :

> " The noble Sidney with this last arose,
> That heroë for numbers and for prose,
> That throughly paced our language, as to show
> The plenteous English hand in hand might go
> With Greek and Latin, and did first reduce
> Our tongue from Lilly's writing then in use ;
> Talking of stones, stars, plants, of fishes, flies,
> Playing with words and idle similes.
> As the English apes, and very zanies be,
> Of everything that they do hear and see ;
> So imitating his ridiculous tricks,
> They speak and write all like mere lunaticks."
>
> (See further, Nares's Glossary, sub voce " Euphuism.")

This fashion of talking " Sir Philip Sidney " has its parallel in the literature of France, where the Romances of Mad. Scuderie, authoress of Ibrahim ou L'Illustre Bassa, Artamenes ou Le Grand Cyrus, &c. brought into vogue the long and inflated compliments of her characters, a folly which is thus satirised by Boileau :—

> " Deux nobles Campagnards, grands lecteurs des Romans,
> M'ont dit tout Cyrus dans leurs longs complimens."

NO. CXVI.—DECISION VERSUS DECIDING.

It was said of one Chancellor (Egertòn I thinke) of a piercing judgment and quick dispatch, that he ended causes without hearing; but of
another .... who was dull, slow, and delatorie, that he heard them
without end.   *L'Estrange, No. 489. Mr. Windham.*

Egerton was a man of no great brilliancy, but sedulous in the performance of his duties, anxious to do justice, and, by long practice, rendered acute in the application of the principles of
equity.   His favourite saying was, " frost and fraud end in foul ; " and, in his character of
judge, he no doubt did what he could to make good the latter part of his *dictum.*   In Bishop
Goodman's lately published " Court of King James," i. 273, et seq. we meet with some
curious particulars of his private history, while by the kindness of his descendant, the noble
President of the Camden Society, the members will shortly be put in possession of materials
illustrative alike of the Lord Keeper's public history, and of the times in which he lived.

Camden, in his " Remaines," (edit. 1637, p. 174), preserves the following anagram upon
his name, " THOMAS EGERTON GESTAT HONOREM."

            " Oris honore viget, vi mentis gestat honorem
            Juris Egertonus dignus honore coli."

NO. CXVII.—A POOR NOBLEMAN.

Sir Jostlin Percy, being told that the Councell had fined him 1000
markes, laught exceedingly at it.   One askt him the reason.   He
answered, that " the Privy Councell were so wise as they knew where
to find 1000 markes ; for hang me if I know where to find 1000 pence,"
sayes he.   *L'Estrange, No. 490. Sir Jo. Pooly.*

Sir Josceline Percy was the seventh son of Henry eighth Earl of Northumberland ; he was
born in 1578, and knighted in 1599.   Having been an adherent of the Earl of Essex, together
with his elder brother Sir Charles Percy, they both received the royal pardon in 44 Elizabeth,
for any concern they might have had in that Earl's rebellion. The name of Sir Josceline does not
occur in the court history of James I. ; the whole house of Percy having fallen into disgrace,
together with Sir Josceline's eldest brother the Earl, on account of the Gunpowder Treason.
He died unmarried in 1631. Sir Josceline seems to have imagined, that the Council acted upon
the rule layed down in Magna Charta, that a man should only be fined *salvo contenemento,*
that is, saving to a freeholder his freehold, to a merchant his merchandise, to a rustic his
plough, to a soldier his arms, and to a scholar his books.   But the practice of the Council was
as much at variance with Magna Charta as their authority, and many members of the Percy
family had sufficient reason to know that it was so.   The Earl was fined in the Star Chamber
£30,000, besides being sentenced to imprisonment for life, and he actually paid £20,000,

and was confined for fifteen years. From the following anecdote, which also occurs in the L'Estrange MS. it would seem, that Sir Josceline was one of the "roysterers" of his day, "Sir Jostlin Piercy, one time when he was drunke, hired a porter to carry him to his lodging in his baskett; so the porter tumbled him in and sett him down at his lodging doore in the baskett, desiring the people to keepe off for the man had the sicknesse, meaning the *falling* sicknesse; whereupon all the streame of people hurryed to the other side of the streete, and he finding his opportunitie, crawl'd out into his lodging."

The plague was colloquially called "the sickness," but the porter here meant only the *falling* sickness. In No. 167 of the MS. we have another story, in which a porter is hired to carry home a drunken apothecary in his basket. It would seem from these anecdotes, that the incident in the Merry Wives of Windsor was not very far fetched.

NO. CXVII*.—A QUEEN AT A DISCOUNT.

As Queen Elizabeth passed the streets in state one in the crowde cried first, "God blesse your *Royall* Majestie!" and then, "God blesse your *Noble* Grace!" "Why, how now," sayes the queene, "am I tenne groates worse than I was e'en now."

L'Estrange, No. 492. *Mr. Windham.*

Ten groats was the difference between the value of the old "ryal," or "royal," and "the noble:" the former passing for 10s. and the latter for 6s. 8d. Our ancestors used anciently to reckon by the mark, which was 13s. 4d. instead of the pound, and the value of all their coins was consequently fixed with a view to computations by the mark.

This anecdote shows the period of the change from the term "your Grace" to "your Majesty," as addressed to the English sovereign. The former title had been customary in the earlier Tudor reigns, the latter became exclusively used shortly after the accession of the House of Stuart, and has since maintained its ground. The Emperor Charles the Fifth was the first crowned head that assumed the appellation of "Majesty," which was soon afterwards adopted by the other European Sovereigns.

NO. CXVIII.—EXERCISE BEFORE BREAKFAST.

Taverner, the great sword-man, to a friend that seem'd to wonder he came well off from so many dangers, "Pish," sayes he, "I can goe out in a morning and fight halfe a douzen duells, and come in againe with a very good stomach to my breakfast."

L'Estrange, No. 495. *Sir Jo. Pooly.*

NO. CXIX.—ARCHEE, THE JESTER.

King James was complaining one time of the leannesse of his Hunting Horse, and swore by his sole he could see no reason but his should be as fat as any of his subjects ; for he bestow'd upon him as good feeding, keeping, and as easy riding as any one did, and yet the jade was leane. Archee, his foole, standing by, told him, " If that be all, take no care : I 'll teach your Majestie a way to raise his fleshe presently ; and if he be not as fat as ever he wallow, you shall ride me." " I pr'y thee, foole, how ? " sayd the King. " Why, doe but make him a Bishoppe, and I 'le warrant you," sayes Archee.

L'Estrange, No. 497. *Thacker.*

Archibald Armstrong, of Arthuret, in Cumberland, was the recognised jester of James the First, who allowed his tongue full license. Archee continued in this post on the accession of Charles I. but lost it in 1637, in consequence of his insulting Archbishop Laud in his way to the council table ; and Rushworth, in his Historical Collections, pt. ii. pp. 470-1, has preserved the instrument by which the King in Council banished Armstrong from the Court, and deprived him of his office.

Mr. Garrard, in a letter to Lord Strafford, describes his fall thus : " Archy is fallen into a great misfortune, a fool he would be, but a foul mouthed knave he hath proved himself ; being at a tavern in Westminster, drunk as he saith himself, he was speaking of the Scottish business, he fell a railing on my Lord of Canterbury, said he was a monk, a rogue, and a traitor. Of this his Grace complained at Council, the King being present, it was ordered he should be carried to the porter's lodge, his coat pulled over his ears, and kicked out of the Court, never to enter within the gates, and to be called into the Star Chamber. The first part is done, but my Lord of Canterbury hath interceded to the King, that there it should end. There is a new fool in his place, Muckle John ; but he will ne'er be so rich, for he cannot abide money."

Archee, indeed, had made a considerable fortune during his residence at Court—

" Archee, by kings and princes grac'd of late,
Jested himself into a fair estate ; "

but being disgraced for his jests upon the " Scottish business," that is, the introduction of the Liturgy into Scotland (one of which jests was his calling the stool flung at the dean, who read the Liturgy in Edinburgh, *the stool of repentance,*) he retired into Cumberland, and dying at Arthuret in 1672, was buried, appropriately enough, on the first of April ! Many curious particulars of his life and sayings, collected by the late Octavius Gilchrist, will be found in the London Magazine for September 1824, from which the above notice has in some measure been derived.

NO. CXX.—" HER MAJESTY THE QUEEN IS IN A PASSION."

Queene Elizabeth, being a little indispos'd one time in her temper, in comes one of her peeres into the Presence : she observing more jollity than usuall in his fashion and discourse, askt him where he had been ? " Y' faith, madame," sayes hee, " drinking your health." " So I thought," sayes she, " and I am sorry for't; for I have observed I never fare worse than when my health is drunk."

L'Estrange, No. 499. *Sir Fr. Needham.*

NO. CXXI.—RAWLEIGH'S OPINION OF A SCOTCHMAN.

Sir Walter Raleigh being at tables with a Scotchman, and having bound him up so as he had but one throw to get out, the Scott threw it, and for joy fell a frisking and scratching, and *clawing his fingers.* At whose fortunate cast and jollity Raleigh was as much moved with indignation, and swore that now he saw it was impossible to bind a Scotchman up so fast but that he would *breake out* in one place or other.

L'Estrange. Sir Fr. Needham.

NO. CXXII.—MUSICAL BUTTONS.

Sir Baptist Hix was telling how his gold buttons were cutt off once in a crowde, and he ne're the wiser (though so much the poorer). Sir Edmund Bacon ask't him if they were not strung upon lutestring? " No," sayes he. " Oh fie then, that was the cause it was not discover'd ; for if they had been strung upon Lute-string, as soone as ever it had been cut it would have cryed, Twang ! "

L'Estrange, No. 504. *Fra. Gaudy.*

A good deal of the wit in this reply consists in its sly allusion to Hicks's trade. He acquired an immense fortune by supplying the Court with rich mercery, and silks ; and no doubt, amongst other things, with " lutestring," or "lustring," as it is sometimes termed. Hicks is celebrated for three things. He gave his two daughters, his coheiresses, 100,000*l.* a.piece as a fortune ; he founded an alms-house at Campden, in Gloucestershire ; and he erected the Sessions House, in Clerkenwell, long known as " Hicks his Hall." Sir Baptist was created Baron Hicks and Viscount Campden on the 5th May 1628, with a limitation of the title in remainder to his son-in-law Edward Lord Noel, who succeeded to it on Sir Baptist's death in the year following.—(Dugdale's Baronage, ii. 462.)

NO. CXXIII.—THE DE REEZ FASHION.

Colonel Morgan, an old souldier, being ask't by an old camerado of his, how chance he was not in the De Reez Fashion ? (in which inauspicious designe the English were most shamefully foil'd) answered, that he lik't it well, and it was very handsome for a man's body, but swore, by God, he did not love to be beaten into a fashion.

L'Estrange, No. 510. *Capt. Hobart.*

The expedition against the island of Rhe was, one would have thought, too unfortunate in its result to have given its name to any fashion. Buckingham returned from it, Hume says, " totally discredited both as an admiral and a general, and bringing no praise with him but the vulgar one of courage and personal bravery." And in a news letter from Mr. Meade to Sir Martin Stuteville, printed by Sir Henry Ellis, in his " Original Letters," (1st series), iii. 251, the action of Rhe is spoken of " as having come to an end with no little dishonour to our nation, excessive charge to our treasury, and great slaughter of our men."

NO. CXXIV.—BETTER AND WORSE.

The Lady Cary us'd to tell Sir John Heydon (for their two witts were ever clashing) that when he was poore, and never a penny in his purse, he was as good company as any was in England, but if thou be'est but 40*s.* strong, there is no dealing with thee upon any tearmes.

L'Estrange, No. 512. *My Mother.*

Lady Cary was Elizabeth, daughter of Sir Hugh Trevannion of Carhayes, in the county of Cornwall, and wife of Sir Robert Cary, a younger son of Henry first Lord Hunsdon. She walked as a lady of the Privy Chamber at the funeral of Queen Anne in 1619 (Progresses of James I. iii. 541) ; and in 1622-3 her husband was created Baron Carey, of Leppington, and in 1626 Earl of Monmouth.

Of Sir John Heydon, the subject of her sarcasms, we have already spoken in our note to No. xliv, where her ladyship is also mentioned.

NO. CXXV.—AN APT DEFINITION.

Thomas Linacre, our English grammarian, being ask't his opinion of Baronius and Bellarmine, though a favorer of their religion in many things, answer'd, that the first syllable of each of their names (BA and BEL) in conjunction, gave the lively character of their persons; men whose scripture and doctrine sounded nothing but confusion.

L'Estrange, No. 519. *Sir J. Pooly.*

This is an excellent story; but is clearly improperly fathered upon Linacre, who died in 1524, whilst Baronius was not born until 1538, and Bellarmine not until 1542.

NO. CXXVI.—A MULTITUDE OF COUNSELLORS, YET NO WISDOM.

One complain'd that Privy Counsellors multiplyed so fast as the table would not hold them. "Why," sayes another, "then some must sitt by like children at joynt-stooles;" for many in King James's time were very green and young. *L'Estrange, No.* 521. *Anon.*

James appears to have been as lavish of honors, titles, and marks of distinction as Elizabeth was sparing of them. His putting up the ranks of the nobility for sale at stated prices, his creation of the order of baronets, and the facility with which he dubbed knights, — no less than three hundred being so created by him in the year 1604,—not only tended to lower the nobility in the estimation of the people, but exposed him to the ridicule of the people, and the jest of some shrewd wag, who affixed an advertisement to the door of St. Paul's Cathedral, offering to teach a new art of memory, which should enable people to recollect the names of all the newly created nobles and knights.

NO. CXXVI*.—FRIGHTENING THE MAIDS OF HONOUR.

The Lord Knolls, in Queen Elizabeth's time, had his lodging at Court, where some of the Ladyes and Maydes of Honour us'd to friske and hey about in the next roome, to his extreame disquiete a nights, though he had often warned them of it; at last he getts one to bolt their owne backe doore, when they were all in one night at their revells, stripps off [to] his shirt, and so with a payre of spectacles on his nose, and Aretine in his hand, comes marching in at a posterne doore of his owne chamber, reading very gravely, full upon the faces of them. Now let the reader judge what a sadd spectacle and pittifull fright these poore creatures endur'd, for he fac't them and often traverst the roome in this posture above an houre. *L'Estrange, No. 530. Phi. Calth.*

The perpetrator of this comical revenge upon the noisy and frolicksome maiden attendants of Elizabeth was probably the celebrated Sir Francis Knollys, K.G. who, as before noticed under No. xxix, married Katharine Cary, the Queen's cousin-german, but was never raised by her Majesty to the dignity of a Peer of Parliament. He is, however, called Lord Knolls in this anecdote, and in No. c. where his name has occurred in connexion with that of Sir Walter Raleigh ; and it is probable that title was frequently given to him, in compliment to his rank as Treasurer of the Household and a Lord of the Privy Council.

Pietro Aretino wrote the memoirs of the most celebrated courtesans of Rome ; and such was the lecture which, according to this very scandalous anecdote, the Treasurer of the Household " gravely " bestowed on the attendants of our Virgin Queen. It presents but a sorry picture of the decency and propriety of the times.

NO. CXXVII.—A RUB AT BOWLES.

The Earle of Pembroke, Lord Chamberlaine, received a disgracefull switch over the face by a Scott (by occasion of the lye), at King James his first comming into England. The impression of which affront, so patiently put up, remained in the memorie of many, a foule staine to his honour. And being at boules in the Spring-Garden afterward, there grew an hott contest between this Lord and Sir Robert Bell about the distance of two boules, and so far that the Lord gave the Knight the lye : Sir Robert startles and stormes about, and in a well dissembled rage (knowing how to wound him deepe without a stroake), cryes out, " Give me a *switch !* " The company smiled, and the conscious Lord scornfully replyes, " And what dare you and that doe ? " " Measure the cast *and beate you*, my Lord, I'le warrant," sayes he.

L'Estrange, No. 535. Mr. Jenkins.

The Earl of Pembroke, to whom this anecdote refers, is Philip the fourth Earl ; and the occurrence took place whilst he was only Earl of Montgomery, during his elder brother's lifetime. It is thus related in a contemporary letter of Mr. John Chamberlaine to Sir Dudley

Carleton, dated 11th March 1611-12 : " On Monday there was a great race or running at Croydon ; where, by occasion of foul play or foul words, one Ramsey a Scotsman struck the Earl of Montgomery with his riding-rod.   Whereupon the whole company was ready to go together by the ears, and like enough to have made a national quarrel.   But for want of weapons it was pacified."   And again the same writer, a fortnight after : " The King was much displeased with the accident that fell out at Croydon, and had the whole matter and manner examined before himself.   Whereupon Ramsey was committed to the Tower, where he is more visited than all the rest, great or small."   (Nichols's Progresses, &c. of King James I. vol. ii. pp. 438, 441.)   This memorable rencontre is also noticed in the Memoirs of Osborne, who says that " Ramsey, by *switching* him on the face at Croydon, rendered him ridiculous.   It was at a horse-race, where many, both Scotch and English, met ; the latter of which did upon this accident draw together with a resolution to make it a national quarrel ; so far as Mr. John Pinchback, though a maimed man, having but the perfect use of two fingers, rode about with his dagger in his hand, crying, ' Let us break our fast with them here, and dine with the rest in London ! '   But Herbert, not offering to strike again, there was nothing lost but the reputation of a gentleman ; in lieu of which, if I am not mistaken, the King made him a knight, a baron, a viscount, and an earl in one day."   It may be concluded, that the resentment cherished against Lord Pembroke by Osborne, and by the Sir Robert Bell of our present anecdote, proceeded, in no small degree, from national prejudice and disappointed malice towards the Scots ; and it should be added, that in the colouring which Osborne gives the story in reference to the King's behaviour, he is here, as elsewhere, grossly, if not wilfully, incorrect.   All the Earl's honours (including the earldom) were more than six years old when the quarrel took place.

Several authors who have noticed the story, as Mr. Lodge, in his Illustrations, Mr. J. P. Wood, in Douglas's Peerage of Scotland, and Sir Egerton Brydges, in Collins's Peerage, have supposed that " Ramsey " was the Viscount Haddington, afterwards Earl of Holderness ; but as Sir John Ramsey was raised to that title in 1606, whilst the antagonist of Lord Montgomery is called only " one Ramsey" by Mr. Chamberlaine, and again by Osborne, he is supposed by Mr. Nichols to have been another person of that name, and most probably William Ramsey, who was a Page of the King's Bedchamber in 1605-6, and appears as a companion of the chivalric exercises of the Prince of Wales at the very period of the Croydon horse-race.   This supposition is confirmed also by Wilson, who in his " Life of James," p. 60, speaks of him as " Ramsay, one of the King's servants."

NO. CXXVIII.—MUSIC WITHOUT WORDS.

One Mr. Saunders, who loved music so well as he could not endure to have it interrupted with the least unseasonable noise, being at a meeting of Fancy Music, only for the Violes and Organ, where many ladyes and gentlewomen resorted, some wanton tongues could not refraine their chatt, and lowd whispers sometime above the instruments. He, impatient of such harsh discords as they often interposed, the lesson being ended, riseth with his Viole from his seate, and soberly addressing himselfe towards them, " Ladyes," sayes he, " this musicke is not vocall, for on my knowledge—these things were never made for words." And after that they had not one word to say.

L'Estrange, No. 536. Mr. Jenkins.

" Concerts of Viols," says Hawkins, iv. 339, " were the usual musical entertainments after the practice of singing madrigals grew into disuse."

NO. CXXIX.—SINGING AT SIGHT.

One Mr. Homes, of the Chappell, who sang very bravely, but had one false eye of glasse, at a meeting for voyces, he standing off from the table, one, in favor to his infirmitie, was removing the deske closer to him, " I pray hold your hand, Sir," sayes he, " that needs not; I see well, and have the advantage of all the company, for if need be (withal pulling out his eye and holding it to) I can bring my eye as neare as I will to the booke." *L'Estranye, No. 543. Mr. Jenkins.*

There is not any mention in Hawkins's History of Music of a Mr. Homes as belonging to the Chapel Royal; but it is there stated, that a Mr. Howes attended as a Gentleman of the Chapel Royal at the coronation of Charles II. and who is probably the person here referred to, though misnamed through a clerical error.

NO. CXXX.—A DRAUGHT HORSE.

A scholler riding his horse hott into the water to drinke, scarce up to the fetlock, one wisht him to goe in deeper (least he foundered his horse); " Hang him, jade," sayes he, " let him drinke up this first." *L'Estrange, No. 546. Mon Pere.*

This anecdote might well pass for one of the Facetiæ of Hierocles; but does not, we believe, figure in that celebrated Collection of Jests, which may, perhaps, be termed the Grecian Joe Miller.

NO. CXXXI.—A GLASS TOO LITTLE.

Capt. Robert Bacon, revelling at Sir W. Paston's, had his sack served him in a curious Venice glasse, but very much under the size that he us'd to trade in. And after a long contemplation of his measure, " Sir William," sayes he, " if you value this glasse (as I beleeve you doe) tye a good long string to it, to draw him up againe, for, before ——, I shall swallow him down at one time or other."

L'Estrange, No. 547. Mr. Neve.

As we have already spoken at some length of Robert Bacon, in the note to No. CXII, our fittest illustration to the present story will, perhaps, be found in a somewhat similar anecdote.

The manager of a Scotch theatre, at which Kean was playing Macbeth, seeing him greatly exhausted towards the close of the performance, offered him some whiskey in a very small thistle-glass, saying at the same time, by way of encouragement, "Take that, Mr. Kean; take that, Sir. It is the real mountain dew; that will never hurt you, Sir!" "No," said Kean, with a significant glance at the *homœopathic* dose, " No ; that I 'll be sworn it would'nt —*if it was vitriol !*"

NO. CXXXII.—A PROFITABLE EXPERIMENT.

A sturdie vagrant, on the high way, begged good-sawcily on Sir Drue Drurie. " Ay, sirrha," sayes he, " such as you make all your kinne fare the worse ; for this is your fashion, deny ye but once (though happily not in earnest), a man's back is no sooner turn'd but ye curse him to the pitt of hell." " Ah, Sir," sayes he, " your worshipp is mistaken in me, I am none of those." " I'faith," sayes Sir Drue, " I'le trye thee for this once," and away he rides.

L'Estrange, No. 548. Capt. Clinch.

NO. CXXXIII.—TOUCHING GREGORY THE HANGMAN.

Some riding upon Tiburne rode, immediately after an execution, and being in discourse of the great difference of the times, and the two potent factions of Presbyterie and Independencie, " I wonder," sayes one merry fellow, "which way Gregorie goes?" " O," sayes a scholler that lov'd to quibble with his witt, " he is for both—consider him in his antiquitie he is Πρεσβυτερος, a Presbyter ; but in his present state and condition (for some of the bodyes were not yet cut downe), *Inde-pendent* out of all doubt." *L'Estrange, No. 551. Anon.*

The subject of the present anecdote was probably only called Gregory, as a matter of custom, as in our own day, the "finisher of the law" (for so this gentlemen is styled according to Old Bailey etiquette) has been commonly known by the name of *Jack Ketch.* Some of our readers may object to Jack Ketch being styled a gentleman, and perhaps in the case of Jack Ketch the objection may be valid ; but it is not so in the case of *Gregory* Brandon (from whom his successors derived their by-name of Gregory) for, as many of our antiquarian friends know, Ralph Brooke, when York Herald, put a trick upon Sir William Segar, Garter King-at-Arms, which had nearly cost them both their places, by procuring a grant of arms to this very Gregory, who thus became a gentleman, and which arms actually appear in Edmondson's Body of Heraldry, annexed to the name of Brandon. The whole history of this very curious affair is fully set forth in the life of Camden, prefixed to his " Britannia," from which it has been transferred to Pegge's " Curialia Miscellanea," p. 334 et seq.

Richard Brandon, who was the executioner of Charles the First, " was the only son of GREGORY Brandon, and claimed the gallows by inheritance."—See Ellis's " Original Letters," second series, iii. 341.

NO. CXXXIV.—WHERE THE WISE MEN CAME FROM.

Sands, a gentleman of a bold spirit and witt, being called to shrift by Lenthall (then Speaker to the House of Commons) and some ridiculous and impertinent interrogatories put to him, was askt at last what countriman he was. " Of Kent," sayes he, " for I will neither blush at my name or native soyle ; and now, Sir, I pray let me demand the same from you?" " I am out of the West," sayes Lenthall. " By my troth," sayes Sands, " so I thought, for I am sure all the *Wise Men* came out of the East." *L'Estrange, No. 564. Frat. Rog.*

William Lenthall, who was a bencher and reader of Lincoln's Inn, was chosen Speaker of the Parliament which met in November 1640, and is known by the various names of " The Republican Parliament," " The Rump Parliament," and " The Long Parliament." He continued to fill the chair until the 20th April 1653, when he was pulled out of it by Harrison, having hesitated to obey Cromwell's command to leave it, a command which the Protector followed up by desiring his soldiers to " take away that fool's bauble," the mace, the insignia of the speakership. He was re-chosen Speaker on the 3d September 1654, being Sunday, which re-election is thus spoken of by Sir Philip Warwick, in his " Memoires," p. 375, " and the old trusty cloak-bag-nag Lenthall (who had kept the chair when sentence was given upon the King), though he was pulled out of his chair by Harrison in the last dissolved Parliament, must now be put in it again, and be made the Speaker of this Parliament."

NO. CXXXV.—TOM BREWER'S NOSE.

Thom: Brewer, my Mus: Servant, through his proneness to good-fellowshippe having attained to a very rich and rubicund nose; being reprov'd by a friend for his too frequent use of strong drinkes and sacke, as very pernicious to that distemper and inflammation in his nose, " Nay, faith," says he, " if it will not endure sack, it is no nose for me."

L'Estrange, No. 578. Mr. Jenkins.

Whether the subject of the present anecdote is to be identified with the author of " The Weeping Lady ; or London like Ninivie in Sack-cloth," 4to, London, 1625 ; and, " A Knot of Fools," London, 4to, 1658 ; or was merely his contemporary and namesake does not appear.

Be this facetious assertor of the qualities indispensable to the most important feature of his face, who he may, he was doubtless " *stuck to his nose*," somewhat like the subject of Quevedo's celebrated sonnet, beginning,

" Erase un hombre a ima nariz pegado ; "

an idea which has been very felicitously rendered into English in the following lines :

Ned is so short, his nose so long,
To say " the nose of Ned " is wrong;
That each may rank in due degree,
" Ned of the Nose," the phrase should be,
Poor Ned belongs to *it*, instead
Of it belonging to *Poor Ned.*

NO. CXXXVI.—POST-MERIDIAN HOURS.

It being found by wofull experience, that many ordinances in Parliament had passed in a most indirect way, at unseasonable houres and thinne houses, to the shame and dishonour of that Royal Councell and ruine of the Kingdome, Sir Benjamin Ruddier (a grave, wise, and a witty man,) stoode up and made this motion, that nothing should be putt to the finall vote upon a thinne House (under a certain number), or after twelve of the clocke ; " for, Mr. Speaker," says he, " we plainly find that Post-Meridian Votes are as dangerous and pernicious as nocturnal lucubrations," reflecting upon their night workes and hellish designes hatched at such unseasonable houres.

L'Estrange, No. 580. *Sr Will. Spring.*

Motions closely similar in terms to the above, are by no means unfrequent in our own times; but they refer to the latter circuit of the clock's daily motion instead of the first,—so completely have our modern habits converted the night of our ancestors into day.

Sir Benjamin Rudyerd was the last Surveyor of the Court of Wards and Liveries, which was abolished in 1646, and of which there is an historical account drawn up by the learned Gresham Professor Ward, in the first volume of the " Vetusta Monumenta," published by the Society of Antiquaries. He was a highly accomplished scholar, and a particularly active member of Parliament throughout the reign of Charles I. endeavouring to moderate the contending politics of the two great parties. So highly was he respected, that, on the abolition of his office in 1642, he was assigned a compensation of £6,000, and a portion of the lands of the Marquis of Worcester. Sir Benjamin was also celebrated as a man of wit and a poet; his Poems were published in 1660, conjointly with those of William Earl of Pembroke, and at an earlier period Ben Jonson had addressed to him three of his Epigrams (cxxi, cxxii, cxxiii), the first beginning :

" Rudyerd, as lesser dames to great ones use,
My lighter comes to kiss thy learned muse," &c.

Sir Benjamin Rudyerd died on the 31st May 1658.

NO. CXXXVII.—AN ILL PROPHECY.

Old Fram: Gawdey, walking with a young gallant in London streets, that us'd to be most vainly prodigall in his habit and dresse, and finding that the splendour of his comrade drew such a goodly traine of beggars, whose broken consort quite confounded the harmonie of their private and then serious discourse ; and perceiving that they would not desist or disperse, after many thundering oaths and execrations from the gallant, Fram: turnes about very soberly, and sayes, "Good people, be quiet, and let the gentleman alone, for hee's a very sociable and sweet-natur'd man ; and I'le be bound hee shall keepe you company within one twelve-month." *L'Estrange, No.* 581. *Sir W. Spring.*

Framlingham Gawdy, esq. of West Herling, Norfolk, was born in 1589, the son of Sir Bassingbourn Gawdy, by Anne, daughter of Sir Charles Framlingham, of Debenham. He was in ward to Sir Robert Knowles, and married Lettice, daughter and coheir of Sir Robert. He was Sheriff of Norfolk in 1627, and died in 1654; leaving William Framlingham Gawdy, esq. his son and heir, who was created a Baronet in 1663.—(Blomefield's Norfolk, 1805, i. 306.)

NO. CXXXVIII.—WORSTED A CRUEL STUFF.

A greate zelote for the Cause, would not allow the Parliament's army to be *beaten* in a certaine fight, but confest he did beleeve they might be *worsted.* To which linsy-wolsey expression, a merry Cavaleere reply'd, "Take heede of that, for worsted is a *cruell* peece of stuffe."
L'Estrange, No. 587. *Anonym.*

Archdeacon Nares, in his Glossary, has remarked, that " *crewel*, a kind of fine worsted, chiefly used for working and embroidering," was a word which " often occasioned puns, from its resemblance to the adjective *cruel;* " and refers to the note on " *cruel* garters," in the Variorum Shakspeare, Lear, act ii. sc. 4.

NO. CXXXIX.—A MOST PROPER SIMILE.

Fra: Russell, at an ordinarie with some of his brethren of Westminster, where much discourse was about the Presbyterian and Independent wayes in religion, borrowed some bold metaphore or allegorie about horse-racing (in which he was well verst), either in the heates or dieting his horse. "Well sayd, Francke," sayes Sir J. Potts, " thy simile is most proper; for thou hast ee'ne as much religion as thy horse." *L'Estrange, No.* 588. *Sir W. Spring.*

" Francke Russell" seems to be Francis Lord Russell, son and heir apparent of Francis the fourth Earl of Bedford, who is well known in the history of the times as a zealous leader of the Parliamentarian side. His son sat in Parliament, but died in France before the Earl, and without children, in 1641.

Sir John Potts, of Mannington in Norfolk, having been previously knighted, was created a Baronet in 1641. He died in 1673 (see his epitaph in Blomefield's Norfolk, 1805, vi. 465.)

NO. CXL.—A LEGAL BULL.

A controversie being at Bury Assizes, about wintering of cattell, before Baron Trevers, then Judge upon the Bench, and the demand being extreame high, " Why, Friend," sayes he, " this is most unreasonable; I wonder thou art not asham'd, for I myself have knowne a beast winter'd one whole summer for a noble." " That was a Bull, my Lord, I beleeve," sayes the fellow; at which ridiculous expression of the judge, and slye retorted jeere of the countryman, the whole court fell into a most profuse laughter.

L'Estrange, No. 597. Mr. Ferrar.

Sir Joseph Trevor, knight, the perpetrator of the legal blunder recorded in this anecdote, was appointed a Baron of the Exchequer on the 10th May 1625.

NO. CXLI.—A GOOD SERMON BAD IN ITS EFFECTS.

A minister, having preached a very long sermon, as his custom was, some hours after ask't a gentleman his approbation of it; he replyed that, " 'Twas very good, but that it had spoyled a goose worth two of it." *L'Estrange, No. 605.* ——

END OF PART THE FIRST.

ANECDOTES AND TRADITIONS.

PART II.

NO. CXLII.—DANCING IN CHURCHES AT CHRISTMAS.

Captⁿ Potter (born in the north of Yorkshire) sayes that in the country churches, at Christmas, in the Holy-daies after Prayers, they will dance in the Church, and as they doe dance they cry, [or sing,]
" Yole, Yole, Yole, &c."

Aubrey, 101 r°.

The practice of dancing in churches, which prevailed among the early Christians, has been by some writers supposed to be an imitation of similar proceedings in Pagan times. The late Mr. Douce, who was of this opinion, quotes in his *" Dance of Death,"* p. 6, a decree of a council held under Pope Eugenius II. in the ninth century, in which the custom is thus noticed : " Ut Sacerdotes admoneant viros ac mulieres, qui festis diebus ad ecclesiam occurrunt, ne *ballando* et turpia verba decantando choros teneant ac ducunt, similitudinem Paganorum peragendo." (Leg. Antiq. iii. 84.)

But may not this practice have arisen among the Jews ? We know that David danced before the Ark, 2 Samuel vi. 14 ; and Eisenmenger, in his *" Entdecktes Judenthum,"* p. i. s. 46, tells us, that it is a rabbinical tradition, that at the marriage of Adam and Eve in Paradise, the Creator and the Angels danced, having the Sun, Moon, and Stars, *als dem Frauenzimmer,* as partners !

A work on the subject of " The Religious Dances of the Early Christians," which I have not been able to consult, but which bears a very high character, I mean, " M. C. H. Brömel's *Fest-Tanzen der Ersten Christen.* Jena, 1705," would probably throw great light upon this point.

NO. CXLIII.—THE YULE LOG.

In the west riding of Yorkshire on Xmass Eve, at night, they bring in a large Yule-log, or Xmass block, and set it on fire, and lap their Christmas ale, and sing,

> " Yule, Yule,
>   A pack of new cards and a Xmass stool."
>
> *Aubrey,* 101 r°. *W. K.*

The learned Dr. Jacob Grimm, in his " *Deutsche Mythologie,*" 117, quotes from the " *Mémoires de l'Académie Celtique,*" notices of a similar custom which prevails at Commercy en Lorraine :—

" Le 24 Décembre vers les six heures du soir, chaque famille met à son feu une énorme buche appelée *Souche de Noel.* On defend aux enfans de s'y asseoir, parceque, leur dit on, ils y attraperaient la gale. Notez, qu'il est d'usage dans presque tout le pais, de mettre le bois au foyer dans toute sa longeur, qui est d'environ 4 pieds et de l'y faire brûler par un bout."

A somewhat similar practice obtains at Bonneval :

" La veille de Noel, avant la messe de minuit, on place dans la cheminée de l'appartement le plus habité une *buche,* la plus grosse que l'on puisse rencontrer, et qui soit dans le cas de resister pendant trois jours dans le foyer. C'est ce que lui a fait donner le nom de *tréfué,* tréfoué, trois feux."

Among the traditions of Denmark, recorded by Thiele in his " *Danske Folkesagn,*" 3 Sam. s. 102, is the following : " When people at Christmas Eve sit together at table and wish to know who among them will die before the next Christmas, some one goes out quietly and peeps in at the window, and whoever is seen to sit at table without a head will die in the coming year." And from Thiele's note we learn that at Anspach it was believed that, when at Christmas or New Year's Day the tree which had been brought in was lighted, any one had but to look at the shadows of those present to learn who would die in the course of the next year, for their shadows would be seen headless.

NO. CXLIV.—DRESSING THE HOUSE WITH IVY.

In several parts of Oxfordshire, particularly at Lanton, it is the custom for the maid servant to ask the man for Ivy to dress the House, and if the man denies or neglects to fetch in Ivy, the maid steals away a pair of his breeches and nails them up to the gate in the yard, or highway.   *Aubrey,* 101 r°. *W. K.*

The subject of decorating churches and houses with ivy at Christmas, is fully described in Brand's Popular Antiquities, i. 404, of Sir Henry Ellis's excellent edition of that book, and which is the only one referred to in the course of the present work. This notice affords us a curious recognition of the principle of tit for tat, the man having refused the maid *her suit*, she takes her revenge upon *his breeches !*

NO. CXLV.—THE LOVING CUP.

At Danby Wisk, in the north riding of Yorkshire, it is the custom for the parishioners, after receiving the Sacrament, to goe from church directly to the ale-house, and there drink together, as a testimony of charity and friendship.—*Ex ore W. Lester, Armig.*

Aubrey, 101 r°. *W. K.*

This practice, which is so perfectly in unison with the character of a simple-minded people, is clearly allied to one still existing, we mean the drinking from the "Loving Cup," a cere-mony which is yet observed by several of the City Companies when the Courts dine in their halls; though, perhaps, more immediately to the Agapæ, which were, says Aubrey, in this same MS. fo. 121, v°. "Certain Love Feasts used in the primitive Church, where all the congregation met and feasted together after they had received the communion, and those that were rich, brought for themselves and the poore, and all eate together for the increase of mutual love, and for the rich to show their love and charity to the poore."

In Grimm's *Deutsche Mythologie,* 36—38, we have much curious information upon the custom (of pagan origin, but which Christianity never succeeded in out-rooting,) of "*Minne-trinken,*" drinking to the love, or rather memory, of the absent. But the passage is too long to translate, and will not very well admit of curtailment.

NO. CXLVI.—JANUARY WEATHER.

There is a Proverb in Welsh of great antiquity,

Haf hyd gatan
Gaiaf hyd Fay.   *i. e.*

If it be somerly weather till the Kalends of January, it will be winterly weather till the Kalends of May. They look upon this as an oracle.

Aubrey, 102 v°.

There is a more modern version of this Proverb in Ray's Collection.

"If Janiveer Calends be summerly gay,
'T will be winterly weather till the Calends of May."

NO. CXLVII.—FEBRUARY SOWLEGROVE.

The shepherds and vulgar people in South Wilts call Februarie " *Sowlegrove*," and have this proverb of it, *viz.* " Soulegrove sil lew " —February is seldome warme—sil *pro* seld—seldome.

Aubrey, 102 v°.

In Forster's Perennial Calendar, where we are told " Februeer doth cut and shear," are many proverbial expressions, which show,

" hail, rain, and snow,
Are now expected and esteemed no woe."

But neither in Forster, nor in any other writer on the subject, do I find February designated as *Sowlegrove*, which is, however, clearly of Saxon origin, Sol monað being the name given to February in the Menologia.

NO. CXLVIII.—EATING LEEKS IN MARCH.

The vulgar in the west of England doe call the moneth of March *Lide*—a proverbial Rhythm,

" Eate Leekes in Lide, and Ramsins in May,
And all the year after Physitians may play."

Aubrey, 159.

The custom of wearing Leeks in March has been so frequently discussed, that here it need only be referred to ; but we do not know that there exists any other mention of the wholesomeness of eating them in *Lide*, as March is here styled, from the Anglo-Saxon name of this month, *hlyd-monað*, or loud month, from *hlyd* tumultus.—(See Lye and Manning, *sub voce*, and Menol. 71.) Neither are we aware of any other record of Ramsons, i. e. Garlick, being more particularly salutary in May than in any other month. We have in fo. 159 of this same MS. another proverbial recipe, which we believe to be new. " Goode to eat Briars in the Sere Month (August). I believe the word Sere comes from Sirius—in the month of the great Dog," says Aubrey.

NO. CXLIX.—PIPE AND TABOR.

In Herefordshire, and parts of the marshes of Wales, the Tabor and Pipe were exceedingly common. Many beggars beg'd with it, and the peasants danced to it in the churchyard on holydays and holyday-eves. The Tabor is derived from the *Sistrum* of the Romans, who had it from the [*sc.* a brazen or Iron Timbrel] Crotalum, a ring of brass struck with an iron rod, as we play with the Key and Tongues.

Aubrey, 106 v⁰.

The Pipe and Tabor, after contributing to the amusement of the people for centuries in a manner to ensure them the admiration, if not of musicians, at least of all advocates of " the greatest happiness " principle, have at length disappeared from among us, and left behind nothing but a name closely associated with the rural pastimes of the country. Aubrey, who, like too many antiquaries, is for referring the origin of everything to the Romans or the Druids, derives the tabor from the Sistrum of the Romans. The reader, who will take the trouble to consult Schillings's " *Universal Lexicon der Tonkunst,*" under the words " Sistrum " and " Rappel," will soon be convinced of Aubrey's error ; while the same work, *sub voce* " Tamburin," shows us the antiquity of the tabor, from its use (or rather its prototype the timbrel) by Miriam, as an accompaniment to her song and dance of victory after the passage of the Red Sea.—(See Exodus, xv. 20.)

NO. CL.—THE HOLY MAWLE.

The Holy Mawle, which they fancy hung behind the church door, which when the father was seaventie, the sonne might fetch to knock his father in the head, as effete and of no more use.

Aubrey, 109 r⁰.

Aubrey has inserted this memorandum as an illustration of the following lines from Ovid's Fasti, lib. v. :

" Corpora post decies senos qui credidit annos
Missa neci ; sceleris crimine damnat avos ; "

and on the opposite page, after quoting Pomp. Mela, lib. iii. c. de India, " Lex erat Sardæ ut filii patres jam senio confectos fustibus cæderent et interremptos sepelirent." Ælian, lib. iv. c. 1 ; and Heredotus, Thalia, lib. iii. numb. 28, adds, " This old story of the Holy Mawle no doubt was derived from the aforesaid histories ; but disguised (after the old fashion) with the Romancy-way ! " And on f. 181 r⁰, he quotes from Wissenbachii Disputationes, viii. § 29, " Olim Ætatis LX annorum excusabat a muneribus publicis, (Plin. iv. ep. 29), unde Sexagenarii proverbialiter dicuntur Depontari, eo quod suffragium non ferrent."—(Car. Sigon. de Antiq. Jur. cir. Rom. 17.)

In spite, however, of all the erudition which Aubrey has displayed upon the subject of this very repulsive superstition, we suspect, that though " much disguised (after the old fashion) with the Romancy-way," it is connected with some of those personifications of the word Hamar *(Malleus),* with the attributes of death or the evil one, referred to by Grimm, in his

"*Deutsche Mythologie*," s. 124 *et seq.* and which seem again, from another passage in the same work (p. 559), to have somewhat of a biblical foundation.

† Hieronymus, in a letter to Pope Damasus, in which he treats of the parable of the prodigal son, speaks of Malleus as among the names of the devil (Greg. Magn. Oxon, i. 1125), " In Scriptura sacra *Mallei nomine* aliquando Diabolus designatur, per quem nunc delinquentium culpæ feriuntur, aliquando vere percussio cœlestis accipitur * * * * * * nam quia in appellatione Mallei antiquis hostis exprimitur, Propheta testatur, dicens : Quomodo confractus est et contritus Malleus universæ terræ." Jerem. l. 23 ; which is rendered in the English version, " How is the hammer of the whole earth cut asunder and broken ! "

The English reader will bear in mind that in the inscription round the tomb of Edward I. in Westminster Abbey, that monarch is termed " *Malleus Scotorum.*"

NO. CLI.—OF WHISTLING.

The seamen will not endure to have one whistle on shipboard, believing that it rayses winds. On Malvern Hills in Worcestershire, and thereabout, when they fanne their corne, and want wind, they cry, " Youle ! Youle ! Youle ! " to invoke it—which word no doubt is a corruption of Æolus [the god of the winds].

Aubrey, fo. 110 r⁰.

NO. CLII.—ALTARS.

Psalm 78, v. 59. " For they grieved him with their Hill Altars, and provoked him to displeasure with their images." The altars many times in process of time became temples, for unless it had been at first upon such an account, one would wonder to see on how high places severall of our churches are placed, e. g. W. Wickham in Bucks, Winersloe in Wilts, and Pestwood, &c. In the infancy of the Christian religion they kept the old temples with new worship, and also the old festivals with a new Christian name. I remember my old friend Sir W. Dugdale told me his remarque, namely, that most churches dedicated to St. Michael either stood on high ground or else had a very high tower or steeple, as at St. Michael's church in Cornhill. The chapelle on Glastonbury Tower is dedicated to St. Michael. So it is at St. Michael's Mount in Cornwall, and (I think in Bretaigne) in France.

Aubrey repeats this observation, but with a difference, as the Heralds say, fo. 162, r°, where he is treating of high places. " So we have St. Michael's Mount in Cornwall, and in Bretaigne in France is another St. Michael's Mount, whither pilgrims doe much resort, as they did also in the old time, to the chapel on the Mount in Cornwall: We have in several places in England, churches and chapells built on high hills, e. g. at West Wycombe in Bucks, St. Anne's Chapel in Surrey, *cum multis aliis.*

" Mem. Sir W. Dugdale told me, he observed, that where a church or chapel was dedicated to St. Michael, that it either stood on a hill, or else had a high steeple, e. g. St. Michael's in Cornhill.

" Mem. The chapel with the tower called Glastonbury Tor, was dedicated to St. Michael the archangel. He is seated on the top of a pico, like a sugar-loafe, which is higher a good deale than the steeple of our Lady Church at Salisbury."   *Aubrey,* 162 *ro.*

Grimm, in his introduction (xxi), to the work to which I have already so frequently referred, has some very interesting remarks upon the manner in which the early Christians " converted temples into churches, erected chapels on the hills dedicated to the Gods, and founded monasteries in the sacred woods," &c.

M. Le Roux de Lincy, in his introductory volume to " *Le Livre des Légendes* " (the only one which he has yet published), has devoted one chapter to " Traditions of Forest and Hills," in which he quotes a number of traditions relative to the Tombeleine and Mont Saint Michel, referred to in the text, from the very elegant and interesting volume published by M. Raoul in 1833, entitled, " *Histoire Pittoresque du Mont Saint Michel et de Tombeleine,*" &c.

NO. CLIII.—THUNDER.

In time of thunder they invoke St. Barbara. So Sir Geof. Chaucer, speaking of the great hostesse, her guests would cry St. Barbara when she lett off her gun [ginne]. They did ring the great bell at Malmsbury-Abbey, called St. Adelm's Bell, to drive away thunder and lightning. The like is yet used at the abbey of St. Germains in Paris, where they ring the great bell then.   *Aubrey, fo.* 110 r°.

The subject of this paragraph has already been published in Aubrey's " Miscellanies," p. 148, with the exception of that part of it relating to St. Barbara, which certainly affords a curious illustration of the passage in Chaucer, if it be not rather Chaucerian, than Chaucer's.

NO. CLIV.—INVOCATIONS TO SAINTS.

Old Symon Brunsdon, of Winterton Basset in Wilts, he had been parish-clarke there t̄pe Mariæ Reginæ : the tutelar Saint of that church is Saint Katharine; he lived downe till the beginning of King James the First; when the gad flye had happened to sting his oxen or cowes, and made them to run away in that champagne-country, he would run after them crying out praying, " Good Saint Katharine of Winterborne, stay my oxen," &c. We must not imagine that he was the only man who did so heretofore, and the like invocations were made to other Saints and Martyrs. *From my old Cozen Ambrose Brown, of Winterborne Basset.* *Aubrey, f°* 113 r°.

NO. CLV.—ST. OSWALD.

St. Oswalde was slayne by Penda, on the great downe east of Marsfield in Gloucestershire, as you ride to Castle-combe, from whence it is called St. Oswaldes-downe. In these partes, nay as far as Auburne-Chase (and perhaps a greate deale farther), when they pent their sheep in the fold, they did pray to God and St. Oswald to bring the sheep safe to the fold, and in the morning they did pray to God and Saint Oswald to bring their sheep safe from the fold. The countryfolk call St. Oswald, St. Twasole. *Aubrey,* 113 r°.

NO. CLVI.—ST. OSYTH.

In those dayes when they went to bed they did rake up the fire and make a + in the ashes, and pray to God and St. *Sythe* (St. Osythe) to deliver them from fire and from water, and from all misadventure.

Aubrey, 113 r°.

NO. CLVII.—ST. STEPHEN.

When the bread was put into the oven they prayed to God and Saint Stephen to send them a just batch and an even.   *Aubrey,* 113 v⁰.

NO. CLVIII.—DEVOTIONAL FEELINGS IN THE OLDEN TIME.

I remember before the Civill Warrs, ancient people, when they heard the clock strike, were wont to say,

" Lord,, grant that my last houre may be my best houre."

They had some pious ejaculation too, when the cock did crow, which did put them in mind of the trumpet at the Resurrection.

Aubrey, 114 v⁰.

It is needless here to refer to the various popular superstitions which formerly prevailed on the subject of the crowing of the cock, since Shakspeare has so perfectly embodied them in a passage in Hamlet, which must be familiar to all our readers. The following verse, however, from the celebrated hymn of Prudentius, who lived at the beginning of the fourth century, exhibits so clearly the antiquity of the belief referred to by Aubrey as to call for insertion :—

" Hoc esse signum præscii
Norunt repromissæ spei,
Qua nos soporis liberi
Speramus adventum Dei."

NO. CLIX.—FUNERAL SONG.

At the Funerals in Yorkshire, to this day, they continue the custome of watching and sitting up all night till the body is interred. In the interim some kneel downe and pray (by the corpse), some play at cards, some drinke and take tobacco. [They play likewise at Hott-Cockles.] They have also mimical plays and sports, e. g. they choose a simple young fellow to be a judge, then the suppliants (having first blacked their hands by rubbing them under the bottome of the pott) beseech his LoP and smutt all his face.

*   *   *   *   *   *

The beliefe in Yorkshire was amongst the vulgar (and perhaps is in
part still) that after the person's death the soule went over Whinny
Moor [whin is a furze], and till about 1616 [1624], at the Funeral a
woman came [like a Præfica] and sung this following song.

> This ean night, this ean night,
>   Every night and awle ;
> Fire and fleet* and candlelight,
>   And Christ receive thy sawle.
>
> When thou from hence doest pass away,
>   Every night and awle,
> To Whinny Moor thou comest at last,
>   And Christ receive thy [silly poor] sawle.
>
> If ever thou gave either hosen or shoon,
>   Every night and awle,
> Sitt thee downe and putt them on,
>   And Christ receive thy sawle.
>
> But if hosen or shoon thou never gave nean,
>   Every night and awle,
> The whinnes shall prick thee to the bare bane,
>   And Christ receive thy sawle.
>
> From Whinny-Moor that thou mayst pass,
>   Every night and awle,
> To Brig o' Dread thou comest at last,
>   And Christ receive thy sawle.
>
> From Brig o' Dread, *na brader than a thread,*
>   Every night and awle,

* Water.

To Purgatory fire thou comest at last,
    And Christ receive thy sawle.

If ever thou gave either milke or drinke,
    Every night and awle,
The fire shall never make thee shrink,
    And Christ receive thy sawle.

But if milk nor drink thou never gave nean,
    Every night and awle,
The fire shall burne thee to the bare bane,
    And Christ receive thy sawle.

From Mr. Mawtese, in whose father's youth, about 60 *years since* (*now* 1686), *was sung this song.   Aubrey,* 114 rº.

This remarkable specimen of the funeral dirge has been printed by Sir Henry Ellis, in his edition of Brand, vol. ii. p. 180 ; and also somewhat differently by Sir Walter Scott, in his " *Minstrelsy*," vol. ii. p. 141 ; neither of whom, however, furnishes us with that important passage, as regards the Mythology on which the Song may be said to be founded, which describes the Bridge of Dread as being " *na brader than a thread ;*" which passage, though a marginal addition in Aubrey's MS., is clearly of the same age and authority as the rest of the poem, and therefore deserving of particular notice as identifying the myth with cognate Jewish and Mahomedan fables.

In the remarks which Sir Walter Scott has prefixed to it, after noticing the word *sleet*, in the *refrain*, (for in his version, we read, " Fire and *sleet* and candlelight"), which he supposes to be " corrupted from *selt* or salt," a quantity of which, in compliance with a popular superstition, is usually placed on the breast of a corpse, he proceeds to quote from a MS. in the Cotton Library, Julius, F. vi. 459, (containing an account of Cleveland in Yorkshire, in the reign of Elizabeth,) the following curious illustration of it:

" When any dieth, certaine women sing a song to the dead bodie, reciting the journey that the partye deceased must goe ; and they are of beliefe (such is their fondnesse) that once in their lives it is good to give a pair of new shoes to a poor man, for as much as after this life they are to pass barefoot through a great launde full of thornes and furzen, except, by the meryte of the almes aforesaid, they have redemed the forfeyte ; for at the edge of the launde, an oulde man shall meet them with the same shoes that were given by the partie when he was lyving ; and, after he hath shodde them, dismisseth them to go through thick and thin without scratch or scalle."

After numerous quotations to show that " the mythologic ideas of this dirge are common to various creeds," Sir Walter has given at full length the very minute description of the *Brig o' Dread*, from the MS. Legend of "Sir Owain," in which the bridge is described as placed between Paradise and Purgatory.

There occurs, however, in the Preliminary Discourse (pp. 120-1, ed. 1801) which Sale has prefixed to his translation of the Koran, a passage so very curiously illustrative of this peculiar superstition, that I trust I may be excused, if, notwithstanding its great length, I quote it entire.

"The trials being over, and the assembly dissolved, the Mahommedans hold, that those who are to be admitted into Paradise will take the right-hand way, and those who are destined to hell-fire will take the left; but both of them must first pass the bridge, called in Arabic, al Sirât, which they say is laid over the midst of hell, and describe to be finer than a hair and sharper than the edge of a sword, so that it seems very difficult to conceive how any one shall be able to stand upon it; for which reason most of the sect of the Motazalites reject it as a fable; though the orthodox think it a sufficient proof of the truth of this article, that it was seriously affirmed by him, who never asserted a falsehood, meaning their Prophet; who, to add to the difficulty of the passage, has likewise declared this bridge is beset on each side with *briars and hooked thorns*, which will, however, be no impediments to the good, for they shall pass with wonderful ease and swiftness like lightning or the wind, Mohammed and his moslems leading the way; whereas the wicked, what with the slipperiness and extreme narrowness of the path, the entangling of the thorns, and the extinction of the light, which directed the former to Paradise, will soon miss their footing, and fall down headlong into hell, which is gaping beneath them.

"This circumstance Mohammed seems also to have borrowed from the Magians, who teach that, on the last day, all mankind will be obliged to pass a bridge which they call Pûl Chînavad or Chînavar: that is, the straight bridge, leading directly into the other world, on the midst of which they suppose the angels, appointed by God to perform that office, will stand, who will require of every one a strict account of his actions, and weigh them in the manner we have already mentioned. It is true the Jews speak likewise of the Bridge of Hell, which they say is *no broader than a thread;* but then they do not tell us that any shall be obliged to pass it, except the idolaters, who will thence fall into perdition."

Sale's account of this Jewish bridge, "no broader than a thread," is confirmed by Esenmenger, in his "*Entdecktes Judenthum*," ii. s. 258.

Notwithstanding the great length to which this note has already extended, I cannot bring it to a close without referring the reader to that very curious chapter (xxi), in Grimm's "*Deutsche Mythologie*," in which he treats of the "Soul"; more especially to that part of it, which relates to the soul's passage across the gulf which separates this world from the infernal regions, wherein mention is made of its "traversing *the bridge across the river*." See page 483; more particularly with respect to the dirge which has called forth these remarks, the passage in which he speaks of the *Todtenschuh*, or shoe of the dead, (in the old Norse tongue, Helskô,) which was bound on the foot of the deceased as a preparation for the long journey on which he was setting forth; and from which custom, although now no longer observed, the honours paid to the dead are at Henneberg, and many other places, still designated as the "*Todtenschuh*."

NO. CLX.—WELL-FLOWERING.

The Fellows of New College have, time out of mind, every Holy Thursday, betwixt the hours of eight and nine, gonne to the Hospitall called Bart'lemews, neer Oxford, when they retire into the chapell and certaine prayers are read, and an antheme sung : from thence they goe to the upper end of the grove adjoyning to the chapell (the way being before hand strewed with flowers by the poor people of the Hospitall), they place themselves round about the well there, where they warble forth melodiously a song of three, four, or five parts.   Which being performed they refresh themselves with a morning's draught there, and retire to Oxford before sermon.   *Aubrey, fo.* 114 v°. *(A. Wood.)*

In processions they used to read a Ghospell at the Springs to blesse them; which hath been discontinued at Sunnywell in Berkshire but since 1688.   *Aubrey,* 115 rec°.

The custom which Aubrey has here recorded, on the authority of Anthony Wood, is clearly one whose origin may be traced to the times of Paganism, and as such, it affords us a striking example of the manner in which the rites of heathenism were eventually christianised, when it was found that they had taken so strong a hold upon the affections of the people, that the decrees of councils and the sermons of the priesthood were in vain directed against them. Grimm's "*Deutsche Mythologie,*" pp. 68, 70, and 326-334, contains an abundance of curious materials illustrative of the veneration in which certain fountains, springs, and streams were formerly held, and of the various peculiar customs to which this feeling has given rise. And in Sir Henry Ellis's edition of "*Brand's Popular Antiquities,*" ii. 266 and 267, a number of similar particulars are collected, in illustration of the following passage, which we quote as having peculiar reference to Aubrey's memorandum on the subject of "*Well-Worship:*"

"Various rites appear to have been performed on Holy Thursday at Wells in different parts of the kingdom, such as decorating them with boughs of trees, garlands of tulips, and other flowers placed in various fancied devices.   In some places, indeed, it was the custom, after prayers for the day at the church, for the clergyman and singers even to pray and sing psalms at the well."

The custom of well-flowering is still practised on Holy Thursday at Tissington in Derbyshire; see Lysons's Magna Britannia, vol. v. p. ccxli : "There is service in the church on that day, and a sermon, after which each of the wells is visited, and the three psalms for the day, with the Epistle and Gospel, are read ; one at each well, of which there are five, of remarkably clear water." See also that agreeable miscellany, Hone's *Every Day Book*, ii. 640, where the correspondent, after giving an account of the Tissington Well-Flowering, refers to the ancient practice of sprinkling the Severn with flowers,—a practice alluded to by Dyer, in his Poem of the *Fleece*, and by Milton in his " *Comus :*"

> " The shepherds, at their festivals,
> Carol her good deeds loud in rustic lays,
> And throw sweet garland wreaths into her stream
> Of pansies, pinks, and gaudy daffodils."

NO. CLXI.—BLESSING OF BRINE SPRINGS.

This custome is yearly observed at Droitwich in Worcestershire, where, on the day of St Richard [the patron or tutelar Saint of the well, i. e. Salt Well], they keepe holyday, and dresse the well with green boughs and flowers. One yeare, sc. aº 46, in the Presbyterian time, it was discontinued in the civil warres ; and after that the springe shranke up, or dried up for some time ; so afterwards they revived their annual custom (notwithstanding the power of the parliament and soldiers), and the salt water returned again and still continues. This St Richard was a person of great estate in these parts ; and a briske young fellow that would ride over hedge and ditch, and at length became a very devout man, and after his decease was canonized for a saint. See his life in an old printed book in folio in the librarie of Westminster Abbey. The day of the solemnization of the Feast and Dressing this Well is the ninth day after Whitsunday.

Aubrey, 142 vº. *From Mrs. Hemmings.*

In Partridge's History of Nantwich, 1774, p. 59, is the following account of a similar custom which prevailed at that place : " Every Ascension Day, our pious ancestors sung a hymn of thanksgiving for the blessing of the Brine. That ancient pit, called the Old Biat, (ever held in great veneration by the townspeople,) was on that day bedecked and adorned with green boughs, flowers, and ribbands, and the young people had music and danced round it ; which custom of dancing, and adorning the pit, continued till a very few years ago."

Klemm, in his " *Handbuch der Germanischen Alterthumskunde,*" p. 338, tells us that among the old Germanic tribes salt springs were considered as sacred, and the wish to possess them led to frequent contests and bloodshed.

NO. CLXII.—READING GOSPELS AT WELLS AND IN CORN FIELDS.

In Cheshire, in Mr. N. Kent's grandmother's time, when they went in Perambulation, they did Blesse the Springs, i. e. they did read a Ghospell at them, and did believe the water was the better.

To this account is added in pencil:

" On Rogation days Gospells were read in the corn-fields here in England untill the Civill Warrs." And White Kennet has added, " Mem. A Gospel read at the head of a barrel in procession, [in the cellar of the Chequers Inn,] within the parish of Stanlake, com. Oxon. Vide Dr. Plot's Natural Hist. of Oxfordshire " [p. 207].

Aubrey, 134 v°.

One of the most ancient forms of well worship consisted in watching at the well throughout the night—the " Waking of the Well," as it is called in a curious satirical song illustrative of some of the ill consequences attendant upon the observance of this practice, and which is printed from a MS. at Cambridge by Mr. Halliwell, in his forthcoming antiquarian miscellany, entitled, " *Reliquiæ Antiquæ.*"

NO. CLXIII.—CLUBS.

In my father's time they had a Clubbe *(fustis)* at the schoole-doore; and when they desired leave *exeundi foras* (two went together still) they carried the clubbe. I have heard that this was used in my time in country schooles before the warres. When monkes or fryars goe out of their convent they always are licensed by couples to be witnesses of one another's actions or behaviour. We use now the word Clubbe for a sodality at a taverne or drinking house. *Aubrey*, 121 r°.

NO. CLXIV.—COCKLE BREAD.

Young wenches have a wanton sport which they call moulding of Cockle-bread, viz. they get upon a table-board, and then gather up their knees and their coates with their hands as high as they can, and then they wabble to and fro, as if they were kneading of dowgh, and say these words, viz.

> My dame is sick and gonne to bed,
> And I'le go mould my Cockle-bread.

I did imagine nothing to have been in this but meer wantonnesse of youth. But I find in Burchardus, in his "Methodus Confitendi," printed at Colon, 1549, (he lived before the Conquest,) one of the Articles (on the VII. Commandment) of interrogating a young woman is, " If she did ever, ' subigere panem clunibus,' and then bake it, and give it to one she loved to eate, " ut in majorem modum exardesceret amor." So here I find it to be a relique of naturall magick—an unlawful philtrum.

White Kennet adds, in a side note,—" In Oxfordshire, the Maids, when they put themselves into the fit posture, sing thus,

> My granny is sick, and now is dead,
> And wee'l goe mould some Cockle Bread,
> Up with my heels and down with my head,
> And this is the way to mould Cockle-bread."

Aubrey, 123 ro.

" Cockell-Bread " is mentioned in Peele's Old Wives Tale; but the ingenious editor of that early dramatist expresses his regret, that " after many inquiries on the subject of Cockell-Bread, he is unable to inform the reader what it was." *Peele's Works,* i. 234. The mystery is now clearly solved; for the question in Burchardus, and which we here quote at length (from Grimm, xxxix), fully establishes the correctness of Aubrey's views as to the origin of this game.

" Fecisti quod quædam mulieres facere solent, prosternunt se in faciem, et discoopertibus natibus jubent, ut supra nudas nates conficiatur panis, et eo decocto tradunt maritis suis ad comedendum. Hoc ideo faciunt ut plus exardescant in amorem illorum."

The rhyme still heard in our nurseries—

> " When I was a little girl, I wash'd my mother's dishes;
> I put my finger in my eye, and pull'd out little fishes—"

is likewise given by Aubrey, with a verbal alteration, and another reference to Burchardus, which serves to establish it as another " relique of natural magick, an unlawful philtrum."

From the following passage in another part of the MS. fo. 161, it would seem as if Cockle-Bread derived its name from the peculiar manner in which it was kneaded.

"I have some reason to believe, that the word Cockle is an old antiquated Norman word, which signifies *nates*, from a beastly rustic kind of play, or abuse, which was used when I was a schoolboy by a Norman gardner that lived at Downton near me.   So Hott Cockles is as much as to say hott or heated buttocks."

The name Hot Cockles is derived by Strutt, in his "*Sports and Pastimes*," p. 393, ed. 1833, (which contains, however, no allusion to any such Norman word as that to which Aubrey refers,) from the "Hautes Coquilles" of the French.   In the "*Memoires de l'Academie Celtique*," tom. iii. we have a description of a curious marriage custom, which may possibly bear some reference to the "*Cockel Bread*," or at least to the etymology of the name.

NO. CLXV.—LEAP CANDLE.

The young girls in and about Oxford have a sport called *Leap Candle*, for which they set a candle in the middle of the room in a candlestick, and then draw up their coats in the form of breaches, and dance over the candle back and forth, with these words,

The Taylor of Bisiter, he has but one eye,

He cannot cut a pair of green Galagaskins if he were to try.

This sport in other parts is called dancing the Candle Rush.

Aubrey, 123 rº.   *(W. K.)*

There is no mention of this sport, or indeed of any one resembling it, in Strutt's *Sports and Pastimes*.

NO. CLXVI.—PAINTED GLASS WINDOWS.

Sir William Dugdale told me, he finds that the art of painting in glasse came first into England in King John's time.

The curious Oriental reds, yellows, blews, and greens in glasse painting, especially when the sun shines, doe much refresh the spirits. After this manner did Dr. R. revive the spirits of a poor distracted gentleman; for, whereas his former physitian shutt up his windows and kept him in utter darknesse, he did open his window lids, and let in the light and filled his windows with glasses of curious tinctures, which the distempered person would alwaies be looking on, and it did conduce to the quieting of his disturbed spirits.

" Johannes Medicus (adds White Kennet in a side note), who lived and wrote in time of Edward II. and was physitian to that king, gives an account of his curing the prince of the small pox, a distemper but lately known in England, by ordering his room, his bed, and his attendants, to be all in scarlet, and imputes the cure in great measure to the vertue of the colour."   *Aubrey,* 127 r⁰.

A French antiquary has recently endeavoured to show that the curious " Oriental reds, yellows, blews, and greens, in glass painting," and other works where such colours appear, are not introduced arbitrarily, or at the mere fancy of the artist, but according to a certain system, in which each colour has its symbolical meaning. See " *Des Couleurs Symboliques dans l'Antiquité, le Moyen-Age, et les Temps Modernes, par* Frederic Portal." 8vo. Paris, 1837.

NO. CLXVII.—PENTALPHA—PENTACLE.

This mark was heretofore used as the signe of the ✠ now, *sc.* at the beginning of letters or bookes, for good-luck's sake ; and the women amongst the Jewes (Dr. Ralph Bathurst tells me) did make this mark on the children's chrysome cloathes.

Mr. Wyld Clarke, merchant (factor) at Santo Crux in Barbarie, tells me that the Jewes in Barbarie have this marke on their trunkes in nailes, and on their cupboards and tables. So in France, &c. and heretofore in England were built crosses for good luck : and my old friend Mr. Lancelot Morehouse, rector of Pertwood, Wilts, was wont to marke this mark at the top of his missive letters, as the Roman Catholiques doe the ✠. And he told me [1660] that the Greeke Christians did so.

"The figure of three triangles, intersected [adds W. Kennet] and made of five lines, is called the Pentangle of Solomon, and when it is delineated in the body of a man it is pretended to touch and point out the five places wherein our Saviour was wounded. And therefore there was an old superstitious conceit that the figure was a *Fuga Demonum*—the devils were afraid of it." *Aubrey,* 129 rᵒ.

The "Pentaculum Salomonis," the "Druden-fus," of the German magical writers, and which is regarded at the present day by the superstitious in Germany as an effective hindrance to the power of witches, is said to have its origin in the secret doctrines of the Pythagoreans, and to have been from thence transferred to the mysteries of Druidism. Be this as it may, it is certain it was looked upon in the Middle Ages as a sign of immense power; and, at the present moment, the Magical Pentalpha, in the western window of the southern aisle of Westminster Abbey, is one of the emblems which still exist, and tell to the initiated, that the black monks, who once chanted in the quire, were deeply read in occult science. We are not, therefore, surprised to find it treated of in Dr. Carl Gräbner's *Bilder der Wunderkunst und des Aberglaubens,* 8vo, Weimar, 1837, p. 86; or that Goethe should have made "*Faust*" avail himself of its influence,

" Fur solche halbe Hollenbrut
Ist *Salomonis Schlussel* gut,"

but it would scarcely be expected, that a belief in its influence should be gravely avowed in a work published at the commencement of the nineteenth century:

" It is always necessary to have this Pentacle in readiness to bind with, in case the spirits should refuse to be obedient, as they can have no power over the exorcist while provided with and fortified by the Pentacle, the virtue of the holy names therein written presiding with wonderful influence over the spirits. It should be made in the day and hour of Mercury, upon parchment made of a kidskin, or virgin, or pure clean-white paper, and the figures and letters wrote in pure gold; and ought to be consecrated and sprinkled (as before often spoken) with holy water.—(Barrett's "*Magus,*" book ii. pt. iii. 109.)

NO. CLXVIII.—CHAUCER'S TREGETOURS.

For I am siker that ther be sciences,
By which men maken divers apparences,
Swiche as thise subtil Tregetoures play.
For oft at festes have I wel herd say
That Tregetoures, within an hall large,
Hade made come in a water and a barge,
And in the halle rowen up and down.
Sometime hath semed come a grim leoun,
And sometimes floures spring as in a mede,
Somtime a vine and grapes white and red,

Somtime a castel al of lime and ston,
And when hem liketh voideth it anon.
Chaucer's Franklein's Tale.

I have heard my grandfather Lyte say, that old father Davis told him, he saw such a thinge doune in a gentleman's hall at Christmas, at or near Durseley in Gloucestershire, about the middle of King Henry the Eighth's reigne. Edmund Wylde, Esq. saies that it is credibly reported that one shewed the now King of France, in anno 1689 or 1690, this trick, sc. to make the apparition of an oake, &c. in a hall, as described by Chaucer: and no conjuration. The King of France gave him (the person) five hundred Louis d'or for it.

M^m. a Hamborough merchant, now (or lately) in London, did see this trick donne at a wedding in Hamborough about 1687, by the same person that shewed it to the King of France. [*E. W. Esq.*]

Aubrey, f° 129.

A much more recent instance of such,

" An apparance ymade by some magike ;
As jogeleurs plaien at these festes grete ; "

is given in the first volume of the " *Gentleman's Magazine*" (1731), p. 79, where we are told, that on the 15th February, "The Algerine Ambassadors went to see Mr. Fawkes, who at their request shew'd them a prospect of Algiers, and raised up an *apple tree*, which bore ripe apples in less than a minute's time, which most of the company tasted of."

This Faux was a well-known character in his day, and fully entitled to be called a " conjuror," since, in the account of his death, which is recorded in the same Magazine, he is said to have died worth £10,000, acquired by his dexterity. Faux may be considered as a legitimate descendant of Pasetes the juggler, described by Agrippa, in his " *Vanity of Arts*," as being " wont to shewe to strangers a very sumptuouse banket ; and when it pleased him, to cause it vanish awaye, al they which sate at the table being disappointed both of mete and drinke."

See also Warton's *History of English Poetry*, ii. 238, who, speaking on the subject of Chaucer's Tregetour, observes, " We frequently read in Romances of illusive appearances framed by magicians, which by the same powers are made suddenly to vanish. To trace the matter home to its true source, these fictions have their origin in a science which professedly made a considerable part of the Arabian learning. In the twelfth century, the number of magical and astrological books translated into Latin, was prodigious." The reader, who is anxious to satisfy himself of the truth of this assertion, may readily do so. In the Collection of " *Early English Prose Romances*," which the Editor of the present volume published some few years since, ample proof of Warton's accuracy may be found. See the "Lyfe of Virgilius," p. 25; "The famous History of Doctor Faustus," pp. 101 and 121; and "the History of Fryer Bacon," p. 29; while among the German legends of "Number Nip," which Busching has collected in his "*Volks-Sagen Marchen und Legenden*," there occurs also a similar scene, and which is translated in Thoms' *Lays and Legends of Germany*, p. 216.

The reader, whose curiosity on the point is not sufficiently gratified by the tediousness we have already bestowed upon him, is referred for further illustration of the subject to Tyrwhitt's notes upon this very passage of the Franklin's Tale, and to Strutt's *Sports and Pastimes*, book iii. cap. iv. Nor will he, perhaps, consider the time thrown away in referring to Luther's "*Table Talk*," in the xxxvith chapter of which he will find a very curious story of a trial of magical skill between the Emperor Frederick, the father of Maximilian, and a conjuror; see p. 390 of the translation published at London in 1652, fol.

CLXIX.—SPAID BITCH.

I believe all over England a Spaied Bitch is accounted wholesome in a house; that is to say they have a strong belief that it *keeps away evil spirits* from haunting of a house. Amongst many other instances, at Cranborn, in Dorset, about 1686, a house was haunted and two tenants successively left the house for that reason; a third came and brought his spaied bitch and was never troubled.   *Aubrey,* 130 vo.

NO. CLXX.—STRIKING A BARGAIN.

In several parts of England, when two persons are driving a bargain, one holds out his right hand and says, "Strike me," and if the other strike, the bargain holds; whence the striking a bargain.

Aubrey, 133 vo.   *W. K.*

A custom somewhat analogous, is said to exist in Westminster School at the present day, where two boys, who agree to fight, go through the form which they call chopping hands; and it is said, that this form of accepting a challenge is looked upon as so irrevocable, that there has scarcely ever occurred an instance of the combat so resolved upon, not taking place.

NO. CLXXI.—WHIPPING OF VILLEINS.

Before Villenage was taken off, if a Lord of a Mannor had whipp't his Villaine to death, he would not have been hanged.

Mem. [adds White Kennet,] A whipping Tom in Kent, who disciplined the wandering maids and women till they were afraid to walk abroad.   *Aubrey*, 136 r⁰.

" *Whipping Tom's Rod for a proud Lady*," is the title of a satirical tract published about the year 1744. Whipping Tom himself would appear to bear some resemblance to Mumbo Jumbo, " who disciplined the wandering maids and women " of Africa.

NO. CLXXII.—DEATH BY ENCHANTMENTS.

King Edward VIth was killed by witchcraft, by figures of wax, see the Chronicles; and the late Duke of Buckingham's mother was killed in Ireland by a figure made with haire, by her second husband (Lord Ancram) brother's nurse, who bewitched her to death, because her foster child [second brother] should inherit the estate. And one Hammond, of Westminster, was hanged, or tryed for his life, about 1641, for killing * * * by a figure of wax.   *Aubrey*, 136 v⁰.

Though there is little authority for Aubrey's assertion, that the death of Edward the Sixth had been compassed " by witchcraft by figures of wax; " and though his supposed union of the Duke of Buckingham's mother with Lord Ancram is so great a blunder, that it is not easy to guess its origin; yet the practice of attempting to destroy the lives of individuals by such a process, was formerly exceedingly common; so much so, indeed, that Dobenek, in his ' *Volksglauben des Deutschen Mittelalters*,' ii. 20-28, devotes a chapter to this peculiar subject.

Shakspeare has perpetuated, in the second part of Henry the Sixth, the charge brought against Eleanor Cobham the Duchess, of conspiring

" With Margery Jourdain, the cunning witch,
And Roger Bolingbroke, the conjuror ; "

that they should, to use the words of Fabyan, " devise an image of wax like unto the King; the which image they dealt so with, that by their devilish incantations and sorcery they intended to bring out of life, little and little, the King's person, as they little and little consumed that image."

Our history affords also many other instances of such attempts ; but the most recent which we have met occurs in Camerarius' '*Dissertationes Physico-Medicæ*,' 8vo. Tubingen, 1712 ; where we have an account of the endeavour of a prisoner at Turin to procure the death of the prince then reigning, by stabbing a waxen image, after he had made use of several superstitious ceremonies, and also of a consecrated host. The man's knowledge, that upon the accession of a new prince to the dominions of Savoy and Piedmont all criminals were set at liberty, induced him to make this attempt, for which, after he had had his flesh torn off with red-hot pincers, he was hanged and quartered. And in the *Memoirs of Literature,* v. 125, whence the above account is derived, we are told that another man had suffered the same punishment for the same crime, at Turin sixty years previously.

NO. CLXXIII.—OLD WIVES' TALES.

In the old ignorant times, before women were readers, the history was handed down from mother to daughter, &c. and William of Malmsbury pickt up his history, from the time of venerable Bede to his time, out of old songs, for there was no writer in England from Bede to him. So my nurse had the history from the Conquest downe to Carl. I. in Ballad.

Before printing, Old Wives' Tales were ingeniose; and since printing came in fashion, till a little before the Civill Warrs, the ordinary sort of people were not taught to reade. Now a days, books are common, and most of the poor people understand letters; and the many good books and variety of turnes of affairs, have putt all the old Fables out of doors. And the divine art of printing and gunpowder have frighted away Robin-good-fellow and the fayries.   *Aubrey,* 141 r°.

This is stated rather too strongly. Malmesbury mentions Bede, the Saxon Chronicle, Ethelward, and Eadmer, as authorities with which he was conversant. Of these, the first and second alone are of much importance for the Saxon periods of our history; and Malmesbury's narrative of that period is principally founded upon them, with some occasional assistance derived, as he acknowledges, from " *cantilenæ,*" old songs ; a source of history not at all to be despised. The mention of this important historian affords me an opportunity of congratulating the lovers of English History upon the prospect of a new edition of his " *De Gestis Regum,*" which, I learn, may soon be expected, under the auspices of the Historical Society. No doubt it will be a worthy companion to their Bede.

NO. CLXXIV.—ST. GEORGE AND THE DRAGON.

The story of St. George does so much resemble this (Metam. iv. fab. 18), that it makes us suspect 'tis but copied from it. Dr. Peter Heylin did write the History of St. George of Cappadocia, which is a very blind business. When I was of Trin. Coll. there was a sale of Mr. Wm. Cartwright's [Poet] bookes, many whereof I had. Amongst others was Dr. Daniel Featly's [he was minister of Lambeth, where he was buried], " Handmayd to Devotion," which was printed shortly after Dr. Heylin's History aforesaid. In the Holyday Devotions, he speaks of St. George, and asserts the story to be fabulous, and that there was never any such man. Wm. Cartwright writes in the margin, " For this assertion was Dr. Featly brought upon his knees before Wm. Laud, Archbishop of Canterbury."

See Sir Thomas Brown's " Vulgar Errors " concerning St. George, where are good remarks. He is of opinion, that the picture of St. George was only emblematical. Methinks the picture of St. George fighting with the Dragon, hath some resemblance of St. Michael fighting with the Devil, who is pourtraied like a Dragon.

Ned. Bagshaw, of Chr. Ch. 1652, shewed me somewhere in Nicephorus Gregor. that the picture of St. George's horse on a wall neighed (quis credere possit) upon some occasion. I don't thinke Dr. Heylin consulted so much Greeke. I will conclude this paragraph with these following verses, that I remember somewhere,

" To save a mayd, St. George the Dragon slew,
    A pretty tale if all is told be true;
    Most say there are no Dragons, and 'tis sayd,
    There was no George; pray God there was a mayd."

But notwithstanding these verses, there was such an one as St. George of Cappadocia, who was made Bishop of Alexandria, and is mentioned by St. Jerome.   *Aubrey*, 142 rᵒ.

Selden has poured out all his learning upon the subject of England's Patron Saint in his " *Titles of Honor*," part ii. cap. v. s. 41 to 44, in which he severally treats " Of the chiefest testimonies in the Eastern parts of Greek Church concerning Saint George."—" The chiefest testimonies concerning him in the Western Church."—" A consideration how he came to be taken for the Patron Saint of the English nation, and of his Feast Day ;" and " Of the

Figure usually representing Saint George; " and where the reader will find ample information upon all the points touched upon in Aubrey's Memorandum.

Selden was inclined to believe, " that his name had been first taken to us under Edward the Third; " but felt some doubts upon the point, seeing that, " in a most ancient Martyrologie, peculiarly belonging to this kingdome, he is the only Saint mentioned for the three and twentieth of Aprill, though both in the Greek and Latin Martyrologies there be divers more beside him on that day. Unlesse there had beene some singular honor given him from this nation, why should his name alone be so honored with it."

The Martyrology to which Selden referred is the Saxon one in the Library of Bennet College, Cambridge.

A striking instance of the esteem in which the Patron Saint of England's soldiery was held at the battle of Poictiers, is given in the curious collection of poems, written by Peter Suchenwirt, the German poet and herald of the fourteenth century.—

> Di Frantzois schrienn " Nater Dam ! "
> Das spricht : Unser Fraw mit nam ;
> Der Engelischen chrey erhal ;
> " Sand Jors : Sand Jors ! " &c.

> The Frenchmen shout forth " Notre Dame,"
> Thus calling on Our Lady's name,
> To which the English host reply,
> " Saint George ! Saint George ! " their battle cry.

See " *Peter Suchenwirt's Werke*," &c. Wien, 1827, p. 60.

NO. CLXXV.—MAZES OR MIZ-MAZES.

The curious description of the Labyrinth [constructed by Dedalus] puts me in mind of that at Woodstock bower, which my nurse was wont to sing,

> Yea Rosamond, fair Rosamond,
> Her name was called so,
> To whom Dame Elenor, our Queen,
> Was known a deadly foe.

> The King therefore, for her defence
> Against the furious Queen,
> At Woodstock builded such a bower,
> The like was never seen.

Most curiously that bower was built
  Of stone and timber strong,
A hundred and fifty dores
  Did to this tower belong.

And they so cunningly contrived,
  With turnings round about,
That none but with a clew of thread
  Could enter in or out.

The Mazes are in imitation of these Labyrinths, and anciently, I believe, there were many of them in England. On the downe between Blandford and Pimpern in Dorset, which was much used by the young people on holidays, and by the schooleboies. At West Ashton in Wilts is another. And I thinke there is one on the Cotteswold Downes, where Mr. Dover's games were celebrated. At Southwarke was a Maze, which is now converted into buildings bearing that name.

There is a Maze at this day in Tuthill Fields, Westminster, and much frequented in the summer time in fair afternoons.

One on Putney Heath in Surrey.   *Aubrey,* 143 r⁰.

The lines quoted by Aubrey are from the ballad (written by the well-known Thomas Deloney, and printed by Percy, *Reliques,* ii. 143), on the subject of " Fair Rosamond," the beautiful mistress of Henry II. who is fabled to have been put to death by Eleanor after she had gained possession of the thread, without the guidance of which it would have been impossible for her to have penetrated the labyrinth or maze by which Henry had surrounded her dwelling place. Brompton (apud *Decem Scriptores,* 1151), has probably furnished the foundation of one part of the legend, who says, " Huic puellæ spectatissimæ fecerat Rex, apud Wodestoke, mirabilis architecturæ cameram operi Dedalino similem, ne forsan a Regina facile deprehenderetur, sed illa cito obiit." But as Sir James Macintosh observes (*History of England,* i. 171), " he speaks only of a contrivance against surprise ; and clearly intimates that Rosamond died a natural death."

NO. CLXXVI.—HORNS.

Mr. Lancelot Morehouse (Westmoreland) told me a story that some-
where in that North countrey, upon an oke were fix't a stagges horne,
which in processe of time grew into the oke; the oke had inclosed the
roote of them; but he had seen the stumpes which weather and time
had curtail'd.   The tradition was that a greyhound had coursed the stag
a matter of xxx miles, and at this place the stagge and greyhound fell
downe both dead; and in a plate of lead was writ thus,

" Here Hercules kill'd Hart of grease,
      And Hart of grease kill'd Hercules."

Horn Church in Essex hath its denomination from the hornes of a
hart that happened to be killed by a king's dogge neer the church as it
was building; and the hornes were putt in the wall of the church.   Mr.
Estest, a gentleman commoner of Trin. Coll. Oxon, went to school there,
and sayd that the stumpes of the hornes were extant in his time.

The Hercules and Hart of Grease is in Whinfield-park, in Westmoreland.   From Mr. Edmund Gibson, of Queen's College, in Oxford,
who is that countryman.   As concerning the time he has not yet fully
informed himself; but he will in some short time and acquaint me.
He intended to have inserted it in his annotations of his Chron. Sax.

The Foresters of the New Forest, in Hants, came annually to St.
Luke's Chapel, at Stoke Verdon, [a hamlet in the parish of Broad
Chalke, in Wilts,] with offerings, that their deer and cattel might be
blest.   I have a conceit that there might be dedicated and hung up in
that chapell (now demolished) some hornes of stagges that were greater
than ordinary.   And the like at St. Luke's Chapel, at Turvey Acton
in Gloucestershire, by the keepers and foresters of Kingswood Forest.

Aubrey, 144 v°. *and* 145 r°.

On the Hart's Horn Tree in Whinfell Park, see the Rev. J. Hodgson's Westmorland, 8vo.
1814 (Beauties of England and Wales), p. 105.   On the various conjectures respecting Horn-
church, see Gent. Mag. xcviii. i. 305.

NO. CLXXVII.—RINGS.

I have seen some rings made for sweet-hearts with a heart enamelled held between two right hands. See an epigramme of George Buchanan, on two rings that were made by Queen Elizabeth's appointment, which being layd one upon the other shewed the like figure. The heart was two diamonds, which joyned made the heart. Queen Elizabeth kept one moietie, and sent the other as a token of her constant friendship to Mary Queen of Scotts: but she cutt off her head for all that.

In the chapell of Priory St. Maries, a nunnery founded by Mawd the Empress, in the parish of Kington St. Michael, in Wiltshire, was found, in 1637, a stone like a grindstone, of about sixteen inches diameter, in the center whereof was a heart held by two right hands.

Aubrey, 146 v°.

Aubrey, who in fo. 234, v°. quotes an old verse as to the wearers of rings,
" Miles, Mercator, Stultus, Maritus, Amator ; "
here alludes, it is presumed, to the diamond ring, originally given by Elizabeth to Mary as a pledge of affection and support, and which Mary commissioned Beatoun to take back to her, when she determined to seek an asylum in England. (See Camden's *Elizabeth,* p. 109, ed. 1615 ; Lingard, viii. 15, ed. 1838.) The following is one of Buchanan's Epigrams on the subject of the ring described by Aubrey (see p. 177 of the edition of his Poems published at St. Andrew's, 1594) :

Loquitur Adamas in cordis effigiem sculptus, quem Maria Elizabethæ Angl. misit.

Quod te jampridem videt, ac amat absens,
Hæc pignus cordis gemma, et imago mei est;
Non est candidior, non est hæc purior illo,
Quamvis dura magis, non mage firma tamen.

And another Epigram entitled, " De Adamante misso a Regina Scotiæ ad Reginam Angliæ," will be found on p. 154 of the same volume.

The carved stone mentioned in Aubrey's latter paragraph is not properly connected with the former subject, but was one of the sepulchral stones placed where the heart of a deceased person was interred apart from the corps.

NO. CLXXVIII.—RHYMERS.

Before the Civil Warres, in Staffordshire and about Coventry, Warwickshire, and those parts, there went along with the fidlers Rymers (who perhaps were fidlers too), that upon any subject given would versjfie extempore halfe an hour together. * * * . These Rymers were of great antiquity in England, as appears by many families called by that name; and like enough the custom was derived from the old bards. In Wales are some bards still, who have a strange gift in ver- syfying; but the fitt will sometimes leave them and never returne again. The vulgar sort of people in Wales here have a humour of singing extempore upon occasion : *e. g.* certain gentlemen coming to ———— the woemen that were washing in the river fell all a singing in Welsh, which was a description of the men and their horses.

Aubrey, 149 r°. *Elias Ashmole.*

NO. CLXXIX.—SORTES VIRGILIANÆ.

In December 1648, King Charles the First, being in great trouble, and prisoner at Caersbroke, or to be brought to London to his triall; Charles Prince of Wales being then at Paris, and in profound sorrow for his father, Mr. Abraham Cowley went to wayte on him. His Highnesse asked him whether he would play at cards to divert his sad thoughts. Mr. Cowley replied he did not care to play at cards; but if his Highness pleased they would use " *Sortes Virgilianæ.*" Mr. Cowley alwaies had a Virgil in his pocket. The Prince accepted the proposal, and prickt his pinne in the fourth booke of the Æneid, at this place.—(iv. 615, et seq.)

> At bello audacis populi vexatus et armis,
> Finibus extorris, complexu avulsus Iüli,
> Auxilium imploret, videatque indigna suorum
> Funera: nec, cùm se sub leges pacis iniquæ
> Tradiderit, regno aut optatâ luce fruatur;
> Sed cadat ante diem, mediâque inhumatus arenâ.

The Prince understood not Latin well, and desired Mr. Cowley to translate the verses, which he did admirably well, and Mr. George Ent (who lived in his house at Chertsey in the great plague, 1665,) shewed me Mr. Cowley's own handwriting.

By a bold people's stubborn arms opprest,
Forced to forsake the land he once possess't,
Torn from his dearest sonne, let him in vain
Seeke help, and see his friends unjustly slain.
Let him to base unequal termes submit,
In hope to save his crown, yet loose both it
And life at once, untimely let him dy,
And on an open stage unburied ly.

Aubrey, who had not at first recovered Cowley's translation, having inserted an extract from Ogilby's Virgil, observes on the last line of the passage he quoted :

" But die before his day, the *sand* his grave."

Now as to the last part, " the sand his grave," I well remember it was frequently and soberly affirmed by officers of the army and grandees, that the body of King Charles the First was privately putt into the sand about White-hall ; and the coffin, which was carried to Windsor, and layd in King Henry 8th vault, was filled with rubbish or brick batts. Mr. Fabian Philips, who adventured his life before the king's trial by printing, assures me, that the king's coffin did cost but six shillings—a plain deale coffin. *Aubrey, f°* 157 *and* 158.

A very different account of the incident related by Aubrey is given by Welwood, in his " *Memoirs*," pp. 93 and 94 (ed. 1820), where it is said that it was the King himself, who being at Oxford, and viewing the public library, was shown a magnificent Virgil, and induced by Lord Falkland to make a trial of his fortune by the *Sortes Virgilianæ*, and opened the book at the passage just referred to. Weldon adds, " It is said King Charles seemed concerned at this accident ; and that the Lord Falkland observing it would likewise try his own fortune in the same manner ; hoping he might fall upon some passage that could have no relation to his case, and thereby divert the King's thoughts from any impression that the other might have made upon him ; but the place that Falkland stumbled upon was yet more suited to his destiny than the other had been to the King's ; being the following expressions of Evander upon the untimely death of his son Pallas, as they are translated by Dryden,

" O Pallas ! thou hast fail'd thy plighted word,
To fight with caution, not to tempt the sword ;

I warn'd thee, but in vain ; for well I knew,
What perils youthful ardour would pursue ;
That boiling blood would carry thee too far ;
Young as thou were 't in dangers, raw to war !
O curst essay of arms, disastrous doom,
Prelude of bloody fields and fights to come ! "

Sir H. Ellis, *Original Letters*, 1st series, iii. 323, remarks upon the manner in which the
King's body was disposed of, " That opinions differed, at the time of this King's death,
respecting his interment cannot be doubted ;" adding, after quoting the above statement from
Aubrey, " Sir Henry Halford's *Account*, however, of what appeared on opening the coffin of
King Charles the First at Windsor, on the 1st of April 1813, has set this question perfectly at
rest."

NO. CLXXX.—VOWING OF CHILDREN.

Mr. George Dickson, now rector of Brampton, near Northampton,
was by his breeding mother devoted to the office of the ministry ; to
which he was bred and ordained, though heir to a plentiful estate.

In the Temple Church at London is a chapel, on the south of the
round about walles, wherein now the fines are conserved, but it was the
chapel dedicated to St. Anne, which was resorted to by barren women ;
and was of great repute for making them " joyful mothers of children."

Aubrey, 162 r°.

NO. CLXXXI.—THE FRIARS MENDICANT.

The Friars Mendicant heretofore would take their opportunity to
come into houses when the good women did bake, and would *read
a Ghospel over the batch,* and the goodwomen would give them a
cake, &c. It should seem by Chaucer's tale that they had a fashion to
beg in rhyme.

Of your white bread I would desire a shiver,
And of your hen the liver.

From old Mr. Frederick Vaughan. Aubrey, f° 178 r°.

NO. CLXXXII.—HARDMEN.

Captain Carlo Fantom, a Croatian, spake thirteen languages, was a Captain under the Earle of Essex.

Sir Robert Pye was his Colonel, who shot at him for not returning a horse which he tooke away before the regiment. Many are living that sawe it; Capt. Hamden was by. The bullets went through his buff-coat, and Capt. H. sawe his shirt on fire. Capt. Carlo Fantom tooke the bullets, and sayd to Sir Robert, " Here, take your bullets again." None of the soldiers would dare to fight with him: they said they would not fight with the devil.

E. W. Esq. was very well acquainted with him, and gave him many a treat; and at last he prevailed with him so far towards the knowledge of this secret, that Fantom told him the keepers in their forests did know a certain herb, which they gave to children, which made them to be shot-free; they call them *Hardmen.* He had a world of cuts about his body with swords; he was very quarrelsome and a great ravisher; he left the Parliament party and went to the King, Charles the First, at Oxford, where he was hanged for ill using women.

This was done in a field near Bedford, where the army then was, as they were marching to the reliefe of Ganesborough.

Robert Earl of Essex, General for the Parliament, had this Captain Fantom in high esteem; for he was an admirable horse-officer, and taught the cavalry of the army the way of fighting with horse. The General saved him from hanging twice for ill using women (once at Winchester, secondly at St. Alban's), and he was not content only to ill use them himselfe, but he would make his soldiers doe it too, and he would stand by and look on.

He met, coming late at night out of the Horse Shoe Tavern in Drury Lane, with a Lieutenant of Colonel Rossiter, who had great jingling spurres on. Said he, " The noise of your spurres doe offend me;

you must come over the kennel, and give me satisfaction." They drew
and pass'd at each other, and the Lieutenant was runne through, and
died in an hour or two, and 'twas not known who killed him.

Said Fantom, "I care not for your Cause; I come to fight for your
halfe-crown and your handsome women. My father was a Roman
Catholique, and so was my grandfather. I have fought for the Christians against the Turkes, and for the Turkes against the Christians."

Mem. Martin Luther, in his Commentaries on the first (or second)
Commandment (I thinke the first), saies that a Hardman was brought
to the Duke of Saxonies Court; he was brought into the great hall,
and there commanded to be shott with a musquet. The bullet drop't
downe, and he had only a blew spott on his skin, where he was struck.
Martin Luther was then by, and sawe the bullet drop downe.

They say that a silver bullet will kill any Hardman, and [he] can be
beaten to death with cudgels. The Elector Palatine, Prince Robert's
brother, did not believe at all that any man could make himself hard.

Aubrey, 202, v°.

Aubrey, who adds to this account the following, "In a Booke of Trialls by Duell (writ by
Segar, I thinke) before the combatants fight, they have an oath administered to them by the
herald ; where is inserted (among other things) that they have not about them either charm or
herb," had previously (fo. 144 v°), inserted a mem. "I have heard from some brokers (that
buy old clothes), that in the time of the civill warres, they found in several cloathes of souldiers they bought *Sigills* of metal, which they wore about them as preservatives." The oath
referred to will be found in Segar's "Honour Militarie and Civill," fol. 1602, p. 134.

The superstition on which the supposed safety of this "bold-faced villain" was founded,
is clearly allied to that which forms the groundwork of *Weber's* beautiful opera, "*Der Freis-
chutz.*" Some traces of it will also be seen in the story of the "Magic Gun," one of
the Palatine legends printed in the *Lays and Legends of Ireland*. In Dr. Carl Gräbner's
"*Bilder der Wunderkunst,*" p. 50, we have, however, a more particular reference to this art
of rendering the body invulnerable. It is there stated to be commonly known as the Pas-
sauish Art, having been first communicated to the German soldiery who were quartered at
Passau in 1611, by the hangman of the town, who gave them scraps of paper to swallow,
inscribed with the mystical signs and words, "*Arios: Beji, Glaji, Ulpke, nalat, nasala, eri
lupie*"; and which, in the belief of the credulous, enabled them, under the command of the
Archduke Matthias, to defeat the ill paid and dispirited forces of his brother the Emperor
Rudolph II.

Another method of accomplishing this object is also related by Gräbner, who, at p. 205, tells us on the authority of Hartmann's " *Teufels-Stucklein*, Frankf. 1678," that a Jew once presented himself before Duke Albrecht of Saxony, and offered him a charm *(Knop)*, engraved with rare signs and characters which should render him invulnerable. The Duke determined to try it, had the Jew led out in the field, with his charm hanging round his neck, he then drew his sword, and at the first thrust *ran the Jew through !*

NO. CLXXXIII.—LENT IS DEAD.

It is the custom for the boys and girls in country schools, in several parts of Oxfordshire, (as Blechington, Weston, Charlton, &c.) at their breaking up in the week before Easter, to goe in a gang from house to house, with little clacks of wood, and when they come to any door there they fall a beating their clacks, and singing this song,

> " Herrings, herrings, white and red,
> Ten a penny, Lent's dead.
> Rise dame and give an egg,
> Or else a piece of bacon.
> One for Peter, two for Paul,
> Three for Jack a Lent's all,
> Away, Lent, away."

They expect from every house some eggs or a piece of bacon, which they carry baskets to receive, and feast upon at the week's end.

At first coming to the door, they all strike up very loud,

> " Herrings, herrings, white and red, &c."

often repeated.

As soon as they receive any largess they begin the chorus,

> " Here sets a good wife,
> Pray God save her life,
> Set her upon a hod,
> And drive her to God."

But if they lose their expectation, and must goe away empty, then with a full cry,

CAMD. SOC. 5.   Q

" Here sits a bad wife,
  The Devil take her life,
  Set her upon a swivell,
  And send her to the Devill."

And in further indignation they commonly cut the latch of the door,
or stop the key-hole with dirt, or leave some more nasty token of displeasure.   *White Kennet. Aubrey,* 206 v°.

The " Jack a'Lent," named in the preceding song, refers to an image so called, which was
formerly thrown at in Lent, like cocks on Shrove Tuesday.   Thus Ben Jonson, in his Tale of
a Tub, says,

———————— " On an Ash Wednesday,
When thou didst stand six weeks *the Jack a'Lent,*
For boys to hurl three throws a penny at thee."

In the introduction to the second volume of " *Kinder und Haus-Märchen*" of the Brothers Grimm, we are told, that in the " Neckarthal," it is the custom for the boys to dress
themselves with paper caps, wooden swords, and sham mustachios, and go from house to
house singing,

" Eier 'raus, Eier 'raus
Der Marder ist im Hühnerhaus ! "

Eggs out ! eggs out ! the polecat 's in the hen-house !
until they receive some eggs, which at night they either eat or sell.

NO. CLXXXIV.—TOM A'BEDLAMS.

Before the Civil Warre I remember Tom a'Bedlams went about a
begging.   They had been such as had been in Bedlam and there recovered, and come to some degree of sobernesse, and when they were
licensed to goe out they had on their lefte arme an armilla of tinne
(printed), about three inches breadth which was sordered on.

Aubrey, 234 v°.

The practice of thus marking the poor " Tom a'Bedlams," resembles that of compelling
the poor lepers of the middle ages to reside in houses set apart for them, and to give notice of
their approach by ringing a bell, or sounding their clap-dish ; a custom which has given rise to
some of the most pathetic incidents introduced into the ballads and songs of the people.   One
of the most striking instances is in the old Dutch song of " Verholen Minne," " Concealed

Love," in which a maiden out of love for a knight, for whom she entertains a passion which he is not aware of, assumes the character of a leper, and resides for seven years in a lazar-house without seeing sun or moon ; her constancy being at length rewarded by the hand of her beloved. See Hoffmann " *Horæ Belgicæ,* pars ii. *Hollandische Volkslieder*," s. 122 et seq.

NO. CLXXXV.—"HO, HO, HO," OF ROBIN GOODFELLOW.

Mr. Lancelot Morehouse did aver to me, *super verbum Sacerdotis,* that he did once heare such a lowd laugh on the other side of a hedge, and was sure that no human lungs could afford such laugh.

Aubrey, 148 vo.

This anecdote of Mr. Lancelot Morehouse, whom the reader will remember, is described in No. clxvii, as " wont to marke this mark [the Pentalpha], at the top of his missive letters," reminds us of Dr. Johnson's belief of having once heard his mother's voice calling " Samuel," when they were many miles asunder.

NO. CLXXXVI.—FAIRIES.

Not far from Sir Bennet Hoskyns there was a labouring man that rose up early every day to go to work, who for a good while together found a ninepence in the way that he went. His wife wondering how he came by so much money, was afraid he got it not honestly, at last he told her ; and afterwards he never found any more.

Aubrey, 166 ro.

Mr. Elias Ashmole sayes, that a Piper at Lichfield was entertayned by the Fayries, who sayd he knew which of the houses of the towne were fayry ground.

Mr. Ashmole also spake of a cavous place, *e. g.* that at * * * * in Surrey, where people, against weddings, &c. bespoke spitts, pewter, &c. and they had it, but were to returne or else they should be never be supplied any more. *Ibid.* 177 vo.

When I was a boy our countrey people would talke much of them. They swept up the harth alwaies at nights, and did sett their shoes by the fire, and many times they should find a three pence in one of them. Mrs. Markey (a daughter of Serjeant Hoskyns, the poet,) told me that her mother did use that custome; and had as much money as made her (or bought her) a little silver cup, thirtie shillings value.

Ibid. 179 v°.

These are acceptable additions to our stock of Fairy Lore. We are told in Busching's "*Volks-Sagen*," s. 331, and Thoms' "*Lays and Legends of Germany*," p. 10, the poor people of Tilleda went to the Kyffhauser mountain to borrow spits, pewter, &c. against weddings. The " cavous place in Surrey," is, we fear, no longer available, and we doubt whether its place is very adequately supplied by the numerous loan societies, whose placards meet the *wall-eye* of the curious reader at all corners of the street.

Sir Bennet Hoskyns, who was created a Baronet in 1676 (the lineal ancestor of the present Sir Hungerford Hoskyns, Bart.), was of Harwood in Herefordshire. He was the son and heir of Serjeant Hoskyns, already noticed in p. 45 ; and Mrs. Markey above mentioned, the wife of John Markey, of Alton, co. Hereford, esq. was his sister.

NO. CLXXXVII.—SELDEN'S TABLE TALK.

Mr. J. Selden writt a 4to booke called Table Talke, which will not endure the test of the presse.   Speaking there of Ovid's Fastorum, he saies, " That he was the Canonist of those times."

The Earle of Abingdon hath a copie of it in MS. as also the Earle of Carbery; it will not endure the presse.

Selden's " *Table Talk* " was first published in 1689, its editor being the Rev. Richard Milward, who had been for many years Selden's amanuensis, and had consequently the most favourable opportunities of becoming acquainted with the sentiments and opinions which he has recorded.

Mr. Johnson, in his " *Life of Selden*," p. 359, from which we derive the above information, quotes a note made by the Earl of Oxford on a MS. copy of this work (Harleian MS. 1315, pl. 426), stating, " this book was given in 168-, by Charles Earl of Dorset, to a bookseller in Fleet Street, to have it printed, but the bookseller delaying to have it done, Mr. Thomas Rymer sold a copy he procured to Mr. Churchill, who printed it ; " and which seems to contradict the former part of his statement.   Mr. Johnson adds, that the authors of the Leipsic " *Acts of the Learned* " disbelieved the genuineness of he book, while Dr. Johnson paid it the high compliment of pronouncing it better than any of the French Ana.   The anecdote related by Aubrey, does not appear to have been before brought under the notice of the reading public.

END OF PART THE SECOND.

ANECDOTES AND TRADITIONS.

PART III.

NO. CLXXXVIII.—PETER PENCE.

Peter pence was an alms granted to the Pope, viz. a peny upon every hearth or chimney, payable at the Feast of St. Peter ad Vincula. This alms was granted only by the King, *ex regali munificentia*, out of his owne demesnes, and it issued only out of such houses as yielded thirty pence rent, *vivæ pecuniæ*. This grant passed at first under the lowly title of an almes, but afterwards it was called *Romescot*, or Romesfeogh, or heord-penny, and the whole summe of it annually amounted but to £200. 06s. 08d. *Collet, p. 9.*

Much curious information relative to the origin of this tax, and its supposed connexion with the celebrated " Schola Saxonum," as well as to the foundation of that institution, will be found in Dr. Lappenberg's valuable " *Geschicte von England*," i. 199; a work which, as it is understood to have found a very able translator in the learned editor of Cædmon, it is to be hoped will ere long be made accessible to the English student.

NO. CLXXXIX.—THE CLERK OF THE MARKET.

The Clerk of the Market (though now a lay person) was originally so called because in the Saxons' time the custody of all weights and measures belonged to the Bishop, who committed the same to some Clerk whom he trusted therewith. *Collet, p. 9.*

NO. CXC.—FARMS.

In the Saxons' time the estates which the Lords of Mannors granted to the freemen were at the first but for years, with a render of a rent, which in those days was of corn or other victual, and thence the *leases* so made were called feormes, or farmes, which word signifieth victualls : but times ensueing turned the victualls into money, and terms of years to terms of life and inheritance, retaining the rents, and those called quit-rents, or the rents of those persons that were acquitted or free.   *Collet, p.* 10.

NO. CXCI.—A PRESENTMENT.

In Henry the Fifth's time the clergy, in their convocation, ordered that three in every parish should make presentment upon oath of such persons as are defamed for hereticks, in obedience whereunto there was a presentment made by some of the parish of St. Mary Overies, in these words, viz. " Item. wee saine that John Stevens is a man wee cannot tell what to make of him, and that he hath books wee know not what they are."   *Collet, p.* 21.

NO. CXCII.—A GOOD REASON.

A picture of the Virgin Mary, which stood in publique view, was made by an artificiall contrivance to appear to weep. This wrought so upon the affections of the spectators, that they all fell to weeping too, except a boy who stood by, and who being reproved for laughing, told them that if they knew as much as he they would laugh too, for hee was sure that this image did not really weep, for hee was servant to him that made this image, and hee did very well remember that hee did when it was making bore a hole in her breech, and if any thing would have made her wept that would.   *Collet, p.* 49.

NO. CXCIII.—ADAM DE ORLETON.

Adam de Orleton, Bishop of Hereford, was indicted of High Treason for aiding the Mortimers with men and armes against King Edward the Second, whereupon he was arraigned, and alleadged "se absque offensa Dei et Sanctæ Ecclesiæ, et absque licentia Domini summi Pontificis, non posse nec debere respondere in hac parte." And thereupon the Archbishops of Canterbury, York, and Dublin, and their suffragans came to the bar, claimed his privilege and took him away. *Collet, p.* 50.

We have here a striking illustration of the manner in which the benefit of clergy (of which we have already treated in our note to No. 1,) was formerly claimed.

Adam de Orleton succeeded to the Bishoprick of Hereford in 1317 ; in 1326 he was appointed Lord High Treasurer of England, which he held, however, but for a short time. In 1327 he was translated to Worcester, and in 1333 to Winchester, which, in the words of William de Edington, its fiftieth Bishop, had " the deepest rack, though not the highest manger."

NO. CXCIV.—A JUSTICE FINED FOR REFINING JUSTICE.

Justice Ingham, in the reign of Edward the First, paid eight hundred marks for a fine, for that a poor man being fined in an action of debt at thirteen shillings four pence, the said justice, being moved with pity, caused the Roll to be razed and made it six shillings eight pence. This case Justice Southcote remembered when Catlyn, Chief Justice of the King's Bench, in the reign of Queen Elizabeth, would have ordered a razure of a roll in the like case, which Southcote utterly denied to assent unto, and said openly that hee meant not to build a clock-house, for, said hee, with the fine that Ingham paied for the like matter the clock-house at Westminster was builded and furnished with a clock, which continueth to this day. *Collet, p.* 52.

The laying out of fines in the erection of buildings does not appear to have been uncommon. In the 9th Henry VIII. Dr. Allan and Sir Christopher Plummer, Doctors of Civil Law, were fined 900 marks, which was ordered to be employed for the building of the rooms from the Court of Star Chamber to the bridge in the palace, and to be paid to Sir John Heyron, who had the charge of the erection. (Archæolog. xxv. 379.)

NO. CXCV.—THE SPREAD EAGLE.

The Eagle with two necks in the Imperial arms, and in the arms of the King of Spain, signifies the East and West Empire, and the extension of their power from the East to the West.   *Collet, p.* 58.

NO. CXCVI.—A JUDGE ON HORSE-BACK.

John Whiddon, a Justice of the King's Bench in the first yeare of Queen Mary, was the first of the judges who rode to Westminster Hall on a horse, for before that time they rode on mules.

Collet, p. 64.

This Judge of horse flesh, for so he showed himself by his preference of a horse to a mule, was John Whydden, Reader, Double Reader and Treasurer of the Inner Temple, who was created Serjeant-at-Law in 1547, King's Serjeant in 1551, and in 1553 (the 1st Mary) was made a Judge of the Queen's Bench. In Thoms' " *Book of the Court*," p. 222, the reader will find a description of the manner in which Wolsey rode to Westminster Hall on his mule, " trapped all in crimson velvet, with a saddle of the same, and gilt stirrups."

NO. CXCVII.—THE JUDGES' ROBES.

The habits of the Judges in antient times having been very various, for certainty and uniformity in them there was a solemn decree and rule made by all the Judges of the Courts at Westminster, bearing date the fourth day of June, anno 1635, Sir John Brampston, Knight, being then Chief Justice of the King's Bench, Sir John Finch, Chief Justice of the Common Pleas, and Sir Humphrey Davenport, Chief Baron of the Exchequer, subscribed by them and the rest of the Judges in those Courts, appointing what robes they should thenceforth use, and at what times, which rule hath been since observed.   *Collet, p.* 67.

A copy of the decree here referred to, is given in Dugdale's " *Origines Juridiciales,*" p. 101, and in Herbert's " *Antiq. of the Inns of Court,*" p. 96. Dugdale has prefixed to it some interesting particulars on the costume of the judges in former times.

NO. CXCVIII.—THE LENGTH OF A LAWYER'S BEARD.

In a Parliament of the Inner Temple, held 5 Maii 1 and 2 Philip and Mary, there was a decree made that no fellow of that house should wear his beard above three weeks growth, upon paine of twenty shillings for-feiture. *Collet, p.* 71.

It may here be necessary to explain, that by a Parliament of the Middle Temple is meant a formal meeting of the benchers of that house for its business, which is always so denominated. (See *Archæologia*, xxi. 107.)

NO. CXCIX.—MIDDLE TEMPLE GATE.

The most antient building now remaining in the Middle Temple is the great gate towards Fleet Street, commonly called the Middle Temple Gate. This was built by Sir Amias Paulet, Knight, about the 7th year of Henry 8, who being sent for up by Cardinal Woolsey, and commanded not to depart London without license, lodged in this gate-house, which he re-edified and sumptuously beautified on the outside with the Cardinal's arms, and other devices, in a glorious manner, thereby hoping to appease his displeasure. *Collet, p.* 71.

NO. CC.—MARCELY HILL.

Not far from Ledborough, in Herefordshire, Marcely Hill rose to an exceeding heighth, and moveing along buried what it met with in the way, continuing that manner for the space of three dayes. *Collet, p.* 87.

NO. CCI.—JACK OF NEWBURY.

John Winscombe, commonly called Jack of Newberry, was the most considerable clothier England ever had. Hee kept one hundred looms in his house, each managed by a man and a boy. Hee feasted King

Henry 8. and his first Queen, Catharine, at his own house in New-berry, now divided into sixteen clothiers houses.   Hee built the church of Newberry from the pulpit westward to the tower.

Collet, p. 113.

The memory of Jack of Newbury, the clothier of England, has been immortalised by the pen of Thomas Deloney, "chronicler," to use the words of Kemp, in his " *Nine Daies Won-der*," of the memorable lives of the " *Six Yeomen of the West*," " *Jack of Newberry*," " *The Gentle Craft*," and " such like honest men, omitted by Stowe, Hollinshed, Grafton, Hall, Froysart, and the rest of those well deserving writers."

The first edition of his " Jack of Newbury " which we can trace, is that in quarto, London, 1633, and which has frequently been re-printed.   A copy of it so abridged as to form " a Penny History," and published in " Aldermary Church Yard, London," is now before us.

NO. CCII.—THE BRERETONS.

It is reported by credible, and believed by discreet persons, that there is a pool adjoining to Brereton, the seat of the honorable family of the Breretons, wherein bodies of trees are seen to swim for certain days together, before the death of any heir of that house.

Collet, p. 115.

NO. CCIII.—THE WARNING POOL.

There is in the parish of North Taunton, near an house called Bath, a pit, but in the winter a pool, not maintained by any spring, but the fall of rain water, and in summer it is commonly dry.   Of this pool it hath been observed that before the death or change of any prince, or some other strange accident of great importance, or any invasion or in-surrection, though in an hot and dry season, it will without any rain overflow its banks, and so continue till that bee past which it prognos-ticated.   It overflowed four times between 1618 and 1648.

Collet, p. 117.

Much curious information on the subject of rivers, &c. which foretell by their rise, or fall the approach of good or evil, will be found in Grimm's " *Deutsche Mythologie*," s. 333.

NO. CCIV.—TWINS.

Nicholas and Andrew Tremaine were twins so like in all lineaments they could not be distinguished but by their severall habits, they felt like paine though at distance, and without any intelligence given they equally desired to walke, travaile, set, sleep, eat, and drinke at the same time, and being souldiers they were both slain together, at New Haven in France, in the year of our Lord 1564.　　*Collet, p.* 118.

NO. CCV.—BONEWELL.

There is a little fountaine called Bonewell, nigh Richard's Castle, in the county of Hereford, the water whereof is allwayes full of bones of little fishes, or as others conceive of little frogs. This spring can never be emptied of them, but as fast as some are drawen out others instantly succeed them.　　*Collet, p.* 121.

NO. CCVI.—JEFFREY HUDSON.

One Jefferey, the late Queen Mother's dwarfe, was son to a proper broad shoulder and chested man. When he was nine years of age hee was scarce a foote and a halfe high. Hee was without any deformity wholly proportionable. Hee was presented in a cold baked pye to King Charles I. at an entertainment. Hee was high in mind, not knowing himself, and hee would not knowe his father, for which by the King's command he was soundly corrected. Hee was a Captain of Horse in the late King's army.　　*Collet, p.* 126.

This "one Jefferey" was, no doubt, the well-known Jeffrey Hudson, who having been served up to table in a cold pie at Burleigh-on-the-Hill, the seat of the Duke of Buckingham, was, as soon as he made his appearance, presented by the Duchess to the Queen, who retained him in her service.—(See Walpole's *Anecdotes of Painting*, ii. 8, 9, 10, &c.) The readers of "*Peveril of the Peak*" need scarcely be reminded of the part which Jeffrey plays in bringing about the denouement of that interesting historical tale.

The custom of keeping dwarfs as appendages to state and royalty was formerly so widely spread, that Flögel, in his "*Geschichte der Hofnarren*," has devoted one chapter to the subject; and to what an extent the practice has prevailed in Russia, the following somewhat lengthy description of the manner in which Fools and Dwarfs are exhibited in the Houses of the Nobles of Moscow will serve to show.

" They are here the pages and the playthings of the great; and, at almost all entertainments, stand for hours by their lord's chair holding his snuff-box or awaiting his commands.   There is scarcely a nobleman in this country who is not possessed of one or more of these frisks of nature; but, in their selection I cannot say that the noblesse display their gallantry, as they choose none but males.

" These little beings are generally the gayest drest persons in the service of their lord, and are attired in a uniform or livery of very costly materials.   In the presence of their owner, their usual station is at his elbow, in the character of a page; and, during his absence, they are then responsible for the cleanliness and combed locks of their companions of the canine species.

" Besides these Lilliputians, many of the nobility keep a fool or two, like the motleys of our court, in the days of Elizabeth, but like in name alone; for their wit, if they ever had any, is swallowed up by indolence.   Savoury sauce and rich repasts, swell their bodies to the most disgusting size; and, lying about in the corners of some splendid saloon, they sleep profoundly till awakened by the command of their lord to amuse the company.   Shaking their enormous bulk, they rise from their trance, and supporting their unwieldly trunks against the wall, drawl out their heavy nonsense with as much grace as the motions of a sloth in the hands of a reptile fancier.   One glance was sufficient for me of these imbruted creatures; and, with something like pleasure, I turned from them to the less humiliating view of human nature in the dwarf.

"The race of these unfortunates is very diminutive in Russia, and very numerous. They are generally well-shaped; and their hands and feet particularly graceful.   Indeed, in the proportion of their figures, we should no where discover them to be flaws in the economy of nature, were it not for a peculiarity of feature and the size of the head, which is commonly exceedingly enlarged.   Take them on the whole, they are such compact, and even pretty little beings, that no idea can be formed of them from the clumsy deformed dwarfs, which are exhibited at our fairs in England.   I cannot say that we need envy Russia this part of her offspring.   It is very curious to observe, how nearly they resemble each other; their features are all so alike, that you might easily imagine, that one pair had spread their progeny over the whole country.''

We have only to add, that further particulars of Jeffrey Hudson may be seen in Hone's " Year Book," p. 16 et seq. where the reader will find also a very neat cut of a Domestic Dwarf, from an engraving in Wierix's Bible, 1594.

NO. CCVII.—WALTER PARSONS.

Walter Parsons, born in Staffordshire, was first apprentice to a Smith, when hee grew so tall in stature that a hole was made for him in the ground, to stand therein up to the knees, so to make him adequate to his fellow-workmen. Hee afterwards was porter to King James. Hee was proportionable in all parts, and had strength equall to his height, valour to his strength, temper to his valour; hee would make nothing to take two of the tallest yeomen of the guard under his arms at once, and order them as hee pleased. *Collet, p.* 128.

A more detailed account of Parsons will be found in Plot's Staffordshire, 1686, p. 294, where we are told that his picture then hung in the Guard-chamber at Whitehall, and another in the great room at the Pope's Head Tavern, Cornhill.

NO. CCVIII.—A LEARNED MAID.

When a learned maid was presented to King James for an English rarity, because shee could speake and write pure Latine, Greek, and Hebrew, the King ask'd,—" but can shee spin?" *Collet, p.* 129.

James appears to have been of Luther's opinion, who, in his " *Divine Discourses at his Table*," &c. Lond. 1651, p. 72, under the head, " What becomes the women ill," says, " There is no gown nor garments that becomes a woman wors then when shee will bee wise."

NO. CCIX.— CARPS.

Carpes are a fish that have not been long naturalized in England, and of all fresh water fishes, the eel excepted, lives longest out of his proper element. They breed severall months in one year, and, though their tongues are counted most delicious meat, yet to speak properly they have no tongues in their mouths, but their mouths are filled with a carneous substance, their teeth being in their throats. There is not one bone in a carpes body which is not forked or divided into two parts at the end thereof. *Collet, p.* 129.

Honest Old Isaak Walton devotes the ninth chapter of his " *Complete Angler*" to the carp; and in this he tells us, " The Carp is the Queen of Rivers; a stately, a good, and a very subtle fish, that was not at first bred, nor hath been long in England, but is now naturalised. It is said, they were brought hither by one Mr. Mascal, a gentleman that then lived at Plumsted, in Sussex, a county that abounds more with this fish than any in this nation."

" You may remember what I told you," Gesner says, " there are no pikes in Spain ; and doubtless there was a time, about a hundred or a few more years ago, when there were no carps in England, as may seem to be affirmed by Sir Richard Baker, in whose Chronicle you may find these verses,

> ' Hops and turkies, carps and beer,
> Came into England all in a year.' "

Some curious instances of the docility of the carp will be found in Walton's fifth chapter, and also in the " *British Angler's Manual,*" lately published by that accomplished artist and skilful angler, T. C. Hofland.

NO. CCX.—KING CHARLES'S PORTER AND DWARF.

William Evans, a Monmouthshire man, porter to King Charles the First, was full two yards and an halfe in height, exceeding Walter Parsons two inches, but far beneath him in equall proportion of body. Hee, dancing in an antimask at Court, drew little Jeffrey the dwarf out of his pocket, first to the wonder, then to the laughter of the beholders.

Collet, p. 134.

In Newgate Street, over the entrance to Bagnio Court, still remains a small sculpture of these two remarkable personages, thus inscribed : " M. P. A. (probably the initials of the builder) THE KING'S PORT^r AND DWARF." Little Jeffrey's height was only three feet nine inches.

The race of tall men is by no means extinct; the tall porter of George the Fourth, who used to look over the gates of Carlton House, must be still remembered.   Monsieur Bibi the French giant, who appeared last winter on the boards of the Adelphi, was another *lengthy* specimen of humanity ; and, lastly, have we not heard lately from America, of a gentleman (probably a descendant from this William Evans, if any of his family ever emigrated to the New Country), who is so tall as to be obliged *to go up a ladder to shave himself !*

END OF THE THIRD PART.

L'ENVOY.

Go FORTH, MY LITTLE BOOK. Thou wilt, I know, find some friendly hands outstretched to give thee welcome. Yet, peradventure thou mayest meet also with unfriendly frowns—kindly meant but hard to bear withal—signs of disapproval from good men and true, amongst whom it is the orthodox opinion that, as antiquarian matters are as old as the Desert, they should be made as dry. Such men may view with displeasure the attempt to treat *old* matters after a *new* fashion: and doubt whether they ought to pardon a heresy so perilous even for the sake of the heretic.

Nevertheless, be of good cheer. Thy course may run more smoothly than he who starts thee on it dares to hope. Farewell, and mayest thou be received in the spirit in which thou art sent forth—as an offering to the *Manes* of William Camden, and as an addition to his *Remains*!

W. J. T.

INDEX.

130

Children, vowing of, 110.

Christmas Block, 81.   Christmas in Denmark, 81.

Churchyard, Thomas, 29.

Civil War, anecdotes of the, xxiv. 50, 78.

Clarke, Mr. Wyld, 97.

Clergy, benefit of, 1. 119.

Clerk of the market, 117.

Cleveland Superstition, 90.

Clinch, Captain, xxvi. 74.

Clock-House at Westminster, 119.

Clock-striking, 89.

Clubs, 94.

Cock-crowing, 89.

Cockle Bread, 95.

Coke, Sir Anthony, 64.

—— Sir Edward, 16, 52.

—— or Cooke, Mr. John, xxviii. 61.

Collins, Dr. 13, 35, 40.

Commercy in Lorraine, 81.

Corbet, Bishop, 30.

Cotteswold Downs, 105.

Cougham, Dr. 20.

Cowley, Abraham, 108.

Cremer, John, 21, 31.

Creswell, Mother, 4.

Cromwell, the Protector Oliver and his family, xiv. xvii.

Crofts, William, D. D. 9.

Cross, origin of the practice of marking infected houses with the sign of the, 33.

Croydon, 14.   Horse race, 72.

Cruel or Crewel, 78.

Cut-purses, 17.

Dalton, Sir John, 43.

Danby Wisk, 82.

Dancing in Churches, 80.

Dandy Prats, the coinage of, 18.

Davenport, Sir H. 120.

Davis, Old Father, 99.

Dean, a Rural, 41.

Death by enchantments, 101.

De Reez Fashion, 69.

Derbyshire, Lead Mine in, 36.

Derham, Mr. 16, 36, 37.

Dickson, Rev. Geo. 110.

Dod, John, the Decalogist, 5.

Dorset, downs in, 105.

Downes, Andrew, 41.

Drake, Sir Francis, 59.

Droitwich, 93.

Drury, Sir Drue, 1, 24, 74.

—— Sir Robert, 31.

Dwarfs, 124.   In Russia, ibid.

Dun, or Donne, Mr. 2, 3, 5.

Edward I. 119.

Edward II. 97, 119.

Edward VI. 101.

Egerton, Lord Chancellor, 65.

Elizabeth, Queen, 16, 29, 47, 66, 68, 107.

Essex, Earl of, 111.

Euphuism, 64.

Evans, William, 126.

Fair Rosamond, 105.

Fairies, 115.

Falling sickness, plague so called, 66.

Fantom, Captain Carlo, 111.

Farms, 118.

Farthings, coinage of, 33.

Faux, the Conjuror, 99.

Featley, Dr. Daniel, 103.

February, Sowlegrove, 83.

Ferrar, Mr. 79.

Field, Dr. Richard, Dean of Gloucester, 8, 13.

Finch, Sir I. 120.

THE END.

LONDON:

J. B. NICHOLS AND SON, PRINTERS, 25, PARLIAMENT STREET.

For EU product safety concerns, contact us at Calle de José Abascal, 56–1°,
28003 Madrid, Spain or eugpsr@cambridge.org.

 www.ingramcontent.com/pod-product-compliance
Ingram Content Group UK Ltd.
Pitfield, Milton Keynes, MK11 3LW, UK
UKHW012341130625
459647UK00009B/436